SRA Reading Mastery

CLASSIC EDITION

Spelling Book

Levels I/II
Fast Cycle

Siegfried Engelmann
Elaine C. Bruner

A Division of The McGraw·Hill Companies

Columbus, Ohio

www.sra4kids.com

SRA/McGraw-Hill

A Division of The McGraw-Hill Companies

Send all inquiries to:
SRA/McGraw-Hill
8787 Orion Place
Columbus, OH 43240-4027

Printed in the United States of America.

ISBN 0-07-569298-8

2 3 4 5 6 7 8 9 IPC 06 05 04 03

Spelling

Note: Do not begin spelling activities with the first reading lesson.

INTRODUCTION

There are 79 spelling lessons in this book. Each lesson takes approximately ten minutes to teach. If you are teaching spelling to small groups, present the first spelling lesson after a group completes lesson 36 in Presentation Book A. If you are teaching spelling to the entire class, you may start after the lowest performing group reaches Lesson 31 in Presentation Book A. Do not include the spelling lesson as part of the reading period.

The children need the following skills to begin the spelling lessons:
1. identifying and writing the various sounds such as **m, t, s;**
2. "saying the sounds" in a word;
3. "saying a word fast."

Overview of Skills Taught

The spelling program is designed so that the children spell by sounds rather than by letter names. That is, they say the sounds in a word, and then write the word.

In the early spelling lessons, the children write single sounds and regular or slightly irregular words (such as **is** and **has**) from dictation. When writing a word, the children usually say the sounds in the word "the hard way"; that is, they pause between the sounds. Then the children write the word.

(Teachers are sometimes concerned that the children will begin pausing between sounds in their reading if pausing is introduced in the spelling. This response does not usually occur. The work with spelling facilitates the children's performance in reading.)

At spelling lesson 47, the children begin spelling irregular words such as **was** and **arm.**

Then at spelling lesson 50, the children start writing an entire sentence from dictation. The children are responsible for remembering how to spell each of the words the right way. After completing the 79 spelling lessons, the children should be placed in *Spelling Mastery,* Level A.

General Procedures

Give each child lined paper and a pencil. Since each lesson takes less than ten lines, you may want to collect the papers and pass them out daily until the page is filled.

Dictated *sounds* and *words* should be written in a column (one below the next).

Depending on the performance of the group, you may be able to teach more than one spelling lesson per day and/or skip every fourth lesson. The criterion for accelerating or skipping is that the children make *very few* errors.

Acceptable Responses

When the children write *words* that have macrons in the reading program (h$\bar{e}$), they should not write the macrons, just the appropriate letters. You may permit them to join letters like **th,** but don't require them to join the letters unless they have trouble writing the word. Children also do not write capital letters.

Examples: Lessons 5, 30, and 75

5	30	75
am	$\bar{e}$	p
sam	me	but
ham	he	that (or **that**)
hit	ham	cat
an	and	will
fan	hand	see
is	mud	this car is tan.
	fit	

Note: Do not begin the spelling activities until the children have completed Lesson 36 in Presentation Book A.

Spelling Lesson 1

WORD WRITING

TASK 1   Children write **it**

a. Everybody, get ready to say the sounds in (pause) **it**. Get ready.
Signal for each sound as the children say *iiit.*

b. Let's do it the hard way. My turn. Saying the sounds in (pause) **it**.
Iii (pause two seconds) **t**. I said the sounds the hard way.

c. Do it with me. Saying the sounds in (pause) **it** the hard way.
Get ready. Signal for each sound as you and the children say **iii**
(pause two seconds) **t**. Repeat until firm.

d. Your turn. All by yourselves. Saying the sounds in (pause) **it**
the hard way. Get ready. Signal for each sound as the children
say *iii* (pause) *t*. The children are to pause between the sounds.
Good.

e. Again. Saying the sounds in (pause) **it** the hard way. Get ready.
Signal for each sound as the children say *iii* (pause) *t.* The
children are to pause two seconds between the sounds.

f. Everybody, write the sounds in (pause) **it**. Check children's
responses. You wrote the word (pause) **it**. What word did you
write? (Signal.) *It.*

TASK 2   Children write **is**

a. You're going to write the word (pause) **is**. When you write the
word (pause) **is**, you write these sounds. **Iii** (pause) **sss**.

b. Say the sounds you write for (pause) **is**. Get ready.
Signal for each sound as the children say *iii* (pause) *sss.* The
children are to pause two seconds between the sounds. Repeat
until firm.

c. Everybody, write the word (pause) **is**. Check children's responses.

TASK 3   Children write **an, am, mat, if, it, in, sin**

a. You're going to write the word **an**. Think about the sounds in
(pause) **an** and write the word. Check children's responses.

To correct	1. Say the sounds in **an**. (Signal.) *Aaannn.*
	2. Say the sounds the hard way. (Signal.) *Aaa* (pause) *nnn.*
	3. Write the word **an**. Check children's responses.

b. Repeat *a* for the following words: **am, mat, if, it, in, sin.**

END OF SPELLING LESSON

Spelling Lesson 2

SOUND WRITING

TASK 1   Children write **h**

a. You're going to write a sound.

b. Here's the sound you're going to write. Listen. **h**.
What sound? (Signal.) *h.*

c. Write **h**. Check children's responses.

WORD WRITING

TASK 2   Children write **is**

a. You're going to write the word (pause) **is**. When you write the
word (pause) **is**, you write these sounds. **Iii** (pause) **sss**.

b. Say the sounds you write for (pause) **is**. Get ready.
Signal for each sound as the children say *iii* (pause) *sss.* The
children are to pause two seconds between the sounds.
Repeat until firm.

c. Everybody, write the word (pause) **is**. Check children's responses.

TASK 3   Children write am, ram

a. You're going to write the word **am**. Think about the sounds in (pause) **am** and write the word. Check children's responses.

To correct	1. Say the sounds in **am**. (Signal.) *Aaammm.* 2. Say the sounds the hard way. (Signal.) *Aaa* (pause) *mmm.* 3. Write the word **am**. Check children's responses.

b. Repeat *a* for **ram**.

TASK 4   Children write if, an, on, it, at

a. You're going to write the word **if**. Think about the sounds in (pause) **if** and write the word. Check children's responses.

To correct	1. Say the sounds in **if**. (Signal.) *Iiifff.* 2. Say the sounds the hard way. (Signal.) *Iii* (pause) *fff.* 3. Write the word **if**. Check children's responses.

b. Repeat *a* for the following words: **an, on, it, at**.

END OF SPELLING LESSON

Spelling Lesson 3

SOUND WRITING

TASK 1   Children write h

a. You're going to write a sound.

b. Here's the sound you're going to write. Listen. **h**.
What sound? (Signal.) *h*.

c. Write **h**. Check children's responses.

WORD WRITING

TASK 2   Children write is

a. You're going to write the word (pause) **is**. When you write the word (pause) **is**, you write these sounds. **Iii** (pause) **sss**.

b. Say the sounds you write for (pause) **is**. Get ready.
Signal for each sound as the children say *iii* (pause) *sss*. The children are to pause two seconds between the sounds. Repeat until firm.

c. Everybody, write the word (pause) **is**. Check children's responses.

TASK 3   Children write at, sat, it, sit, in, sin

a. You're going to write the word **at**. Think about the sounds in (pause) **at** and write the word. Check children's responses.

To correct	1. Say the sounds in **at**. (Signal.) *Aaat.* 2. Say the sounds the hard way. (Signal.) *Aaa* (pause) *t.* 3. Write the word **at**. Check children's responses.

b. Repeat *a* for the following words: **sat, it, sit, in,** and **sin**.

END OF SPELLING LESSON

Spelling Lesson 4

WORD WRITING

TASK 1   Children write it, sit

a. You're going to write the word **it**. Think about the sounds in (pause) **it** and write the word. Check children's responses.

To correct	1. Say the sounds in **it**. (Signal.) *Iiit.* 2. Say the sounds the hard way. (Signal.) *Iii* (pause) *t.* 3. Write the word **it**. Check children's responses.

b. Repeat *a* for **sit**.

TASK 2   Children write **hit**

a. You're going to write the word (pause) **hit**. This word is tough.
I'll say the sounds in (pause) **hit** the hard way. Listen.
H (pause one second) **iii** (pause one second) **t**.
b. Your turn. Say the sounds in (pause) **hit**. Get ready.
Signal for each sound as the children say *h* (pause) *iii* (pause) *t*.
The children are to pause two seconds between the sounds.
Repeat until firm.

c. Everybody, write the word (pause) **hit**. Check children's responses.

TASK 3   Children write **at, fat, rat**

a. You're going to write the word **at**. Think about the sounds in
(pause) **at** and write the word. Check children's responses.
b. Repeat *a* for **fat** and **rat**.

TASK 4   Children write **hat**

a. You're going to write the word (pause) **hat**. This word is tough.
I'll say the sounds in (pause) **hat** the hard way. Listen.
H (pause one second) **aaa** (pause one second) **t**.
b. Your turn. Say the sounds in (pause) **hat**. Get ready.
Signal for each sound as the children say *h* (pause) *aaa* (pause) *t*.
The children are to pause two seconds between sounds. Repeat
until firm.

c. Everybody, write the word (pause) **hat**. Check children's
responses.

TASK 5   Children write **is**

a. You're going to write the word (pause) **is**. When you write the
word (pause) **is**, you write these sounds. **Iii** (pause) **sss**.
b. Say the sounds you write for (pause) **is**. Get ready.
Signal for each sound as the children say *iii* (pause) *sss*. The
children are to pause two seconds between the sounds. Repeat
until firm.

c. Everybody, write the word (pause) **is**. Check children's responses.

END OF SPELLING LESSON

Spelling Lesson 5

WORD WRITING

TASK 1   Children write **am, sam**

a. You're going to write the word **am**. Think about the sounds in
(pause) **am** and write the word. Check children's responses.

To correct	1. Say the sounds in **am**. (Signal.) *Aaammm*.
	2. Say the sounds the hard way. (Signal.) *Aaa* (pause) *mmm*.
	3. Write the word **am**. Check children's responses.

b. Repeat *a* for **sam**.

TASK 2   Children write **ham**

a. You're going to write the word (pause) **ham**. This word is tough.
I'll say the sounds in (pause) **ham** the hard way. Listen.
H (pause one second) **aaa** (pause one second) **mmm**.
b. Your turn. Say the sounds in (pause) **ham**. Get ready.
Signal for each sound as the children say *h* (pause) *aaa* (pause)
mmm. The children are to pause two seconds between the sounds.
Repeat until firm.

c. Everybody, write the word (pause) **ham**. Check responses.

TASK 3   Children write **it**

You're going to write the word **it**. Think about the sounds in (pause)
it and write the word. Check children's responses.

5

TASK 4   Children write hit

a. You're going to write the word (pause) **hit**. This word is tough.
I'll say the sounds in (pause) **hit** the hard way. Listen.
H (pause one second) **iii** (pause one second) **t.**

b. Your turn. Say the sounds in (pause) **hit**. Get ready.
Signal for each sound as the children say *h* (pause) *iii* (pause) *t.*
The children are to pause two seconds between the sounds.
Repeat until firm.

c. Everybody, write the word (pause) **hit**. Check children's responses.

TASK 5   Children write an, fan

a. You're going to write the word **an**. Think about the sounds in
(pause) **an** and write the word. Check children's responses.

b. Repeat *a* for **fan.**

TASK 6   Children write is

a. You're going to write the word (pause) **is**. Say the sounds you
write for (pause) **is**. Get ready. Signal for each sound as the
children say *iii* (pause) *sss.* The children are to pause two seconds
between the sounds. Repeat until firm.

b. Everybody, write the word (pause) **is**. Check children's responses.

END OF SPELLING LESSON

Spelling Lesson 6

WORD WRITING

TASK 1   Children write am

You're going to write the word **am**. Think about the sounds in (pause)
am and write the word. Check children's responses.

To correct	1. Say the sounds in **am**. (Signal.) *Aaammm.*
	2. Say the sounds the hard way. (Signal.) *Aaa* (pause) *mmm.*
	3. Write the word **am**. Check children's responses.

TASK 2   Children write ham

a. You're going to write the word (pause) **ham**. This word is tough.
I'll say the sounds in (pause) **ham** the hard way. Listen.
H (pause one second) **aaa** (pause one second) **mmm.**

b. Your turn. Say the sounds in (pause) **ham**. Get ready.
Signal for each sound as the children say *h* (pause) *aaa* (pause)
mmm. The children are to pause two seconds between the sounds.
Repeat until firm.

c. Everybody, write the word (pause) **ham**. Check responses.

TASK 3   Children write it

You're going to write the word **it**. Think about the sounds in (pause)
it and write the word. Check children's responses.

TASK 4   Children write hit

a. Now you're going to write the word (pause) **hit**. This word is tough.
I'll say the sounds in (pause) **hit** the hard way. Listen.
H (pause one second) **iii** (pause one second) **t.**

b. Your turn. Say the sounds in (pause) **hit**. Get ready.
Signal for each sound as the children say *h* (pause) *iii* (pause) *t.*
The children are to pause two seconds between the sounds.
Repeat until firm.

c. Everybody, write the word (pause) **hit**. Check children's responses.

TASK 5 Children write **is**

a. Everybody, you're going to write the word (pause) **is**. Say the sounds you write for (pause) **is**. Get ready. Signal for each sound as the children say *iii* (pause) *sss.* The children are to pause two seconds between the sounds. Repeat until firm.

b. Everybody, write the word (pause) **is**. Check children's responses.

TASK 6 Children write **his, has**

---

a. You're going to write the word (pause) **his**. When you write the word (pause) **his**, you write these sounds: **H** (pause) **iii** (pause) **sss**.

b. Say the sounds you write for (pause) **his**. Get ready. Signal for each sound as the children say *h* (pause) *iii* (pause) *sss.* The children are to pause two seconds between the sounds. Repeat until firm.

c. Everybody, write the word (pause) **his**. Check responses.

d. You're going to write the word (pause) **has**. When you write the word (pause) **has**, you write these sounds: **H** (pause) **aaa** (pause) **sss**.

e. Say the sounds you write for (pause) **has**. Signal for each sound as the children say *h* (pause) *aaa* (pause) *sss.* The children are to pause two seconds between the sounds. Repeat until firm.

f. Everybody, write the word (pause) **has**. Check responses.

TASK 7 Children write **on**

You're going to write the word **on**. Think about the sounds in (pause) **on** and write the word. Check children's responses.

END OF SPELLING LESSON

Spelling Lesson 7

WORD WRITING

TASK 1 Children write **at**

You're going to write the word **at**. Think about the sounds in (pause) **at** and write the word. Check children's responses.

To correct	1. Say the sounds in **at**. (Signal.) *Aaat.*
	2. Say the sounds the hard way. (Signal.) *Aaa* (pause) *t.*
	3. Write the word **at**. Check children's responses.

TASK 2 Children write **hat**

a. You're going to write the word (pause) **hat**. This word is tough. I'll say the sounds in (pause) **hat** the hard way. Listen. **H** (pause) **aaa** (pause) **t**.

b. Your turn. Say the sounds in (pause) **hat**. Get ready. Signal for each sound as the children say *h* (pause) *aaa* (pause) *t.* The children are to pause two seconds between the sounds. Repeat until firm.

c. Everybody, write the word (pause) **hat**. Check children's responses.

TASK 3 Children write **it**

You're going to write the word **it**. Think about the sounds in (pause) **it** and write the word. Check children's responses.

TASK 4   Children write **hit**

a. You're going to write the word (pause) **hit**. This word is tough.
I'll say the sounds in (pause) **hit** the hard way. Listen.
H (pause) **iii** (pause) **t**.

b. Your turn. Say the sounds in (pause) **hit**. Get ready.
Signal for each sound as the children say *h* (pause) *iii* (pause) *t*.
The children are to pause two seconds between the sounds.
Repeat until firm.

c. Everybody, write the word (pause) **hit**. Check children's
responses.

TASK 5   Children write **is**, **his**

a. You're going to write the word (pause) **is**. Say the sounds you
write for (pause) **is**. Get ready. Signal for each sound as the
children say *iii* (pause) *sss*. The children are to pause two
seconds between the sounds. Repeat until firm.

b. Everybody, write the word (pause) **is**. Check children's responses.

c. Now, you're going to write the word (pause) **his**. Say the sounds
you write for (pause) **his**. Get ready. Signal for each sound as
the children say *h* (pause) *iii* (pause) *sss*. The children are to
pause two seconds between the sounds. Repeat until firm.

d. Everybody, write the word (pause) **his**. Check children's
responses.

TASK 6   Children write **has**

a. You're going to write the word (pause) **has**. When you write the
word (pause) **has**, you write these sounds. **H** (pause) **aaa**
(pause) **sss**.

b. Say the sounds you write for (pause) **has**. Get ready. Signal for
each sound as the children say *h* (pause) *aaa* (pause) *sss*. The
children are to pause two seconds between the sounds. Repeat
until firm.

c. Everybody, write the word (pause) **has**. Check children's
responses.

TASK 7   Children write **ham**

a. You're going to write the word (pause) **ham**. This word is tough.
I'll say the sounds in (pause) **ham** the hard way. Listen.
H (pause) **aaa** (pause) **mmm**

b. Your turn. Say the sounds in (pause) **ham**. Get ready.
Signal for each sound as the children say *h* (pause) *aaa* (pause)
mmm. The children are to pause two seconds between the sounds.
Repeat until firm.

c. Everybody, write the word (pause) **ham**. Check children's
responses.

END OF SPELLING LESSON

Spelling Lesson 8

WORD WRITING

TASK 1   Children write **not, rot**

a. You're going to write the word **not**. Listen. **Not**. Saying the sounds
in (pause) **not** the hard way. Get ready. Signal for each sound
as the children say *nnn* (pause) *ooo* (pause) *t*. The children are to
pause two seconds between the sounds. Repeat until firm.

b. Everybody, write the word (pause) **not**. Check children's
responses.

c. Repeat *a* and *b* for **rot**.

TASK 2   Children write **hot**

a. You're going to write the word (pause) **hot**. This word is tough.
I'll say the sounds in (pause) **hot** the hard way. Listen.
H (pause) **ooo** (pause) **t**.

b. Your turn. Say the sounds in (pause) **hot**. Get ready.
Signal for each sound as the children say *h* (pause) *ooo* (pause) *t*.
The children are to pause two seconds between the sounds.
Repeat until firm.

c. Everybody, write the word (pause) **hot**. Check children's
responses.

TASK 3 Children write rat, fat

a. You're going to write the word **rat**. Think about the sounds in (pause) **rat** and write the word. Check children's responses.

To correct	1. Say the sounds in **rat**. (Signal.) *Rrraaat.*
	2. Say the sounds the hard way. (Signal.) *Rrr* (pause) *aaa* (pause) *t.*
	3. Write the word **rat**. Check children's responses.

b. Repeat *a* for **fat**.

TASK 4 Children write hat

a. You're going to write the word (pause) **hat**. This word is tough. I'll say the sounds in (pause) **hat** the hard way. Listen. **H** (pause) **aaa** (pause) **t**.

b. Your turn. Say the sounds in (pause) **hat**. Get ready.
Signal for each sound as the children say *h* (pause) *aaa* (pause) *t.* The children are to pause two seconds between the sounds. Repeat until firm.

c. Everybody, write the word (pause) **hat**. Check children's responses.

TASK 5 Children write is, his

a. You're going to write the word (pause) **is**. Say the sounds you write for (pause) **is**. Get ready. Signal for each sound as the children say *iii* (pause) *sss.* The children are to pause two seconds between the sounds. Repeat until firm.

b. Everybody, write the word (pause) **is**. Check children's responses.

c. Now, you're going to write the word (pause) **his**. Say the sounds you write for (pause) **his**. Get ready. Signal for each sound as the children say *h* (pause) *iii* (pause) *sss.* The children are to pause two seconds between the sounds. Repeat until firm.

d. Everybody, write the word (pause) **his**. Check children's responses.

END OF SPELLING LESSON

Spelling Lesson 9

WORD WRITING

TASK 1 Children write hat, hot

a. You're going to write the word (pause) **hat**. This word is tough. I'll say the sounds in (pause) **hat** the hard way. Listen. **H** (pause) **aaa** (pause) **t**.

b. Your turn. Say the sounds in (pause) **hat**. Get ready.
Signal for each sound as the children say *h* (pause) *aaa* (pause) *t.* The children are to pause two seconds between the sounds. Repeat until firm.

c. Everybody, write the word (pause) **hat**. Check children's responses.

d. Now, you're going to write the word (pause) **hot**. This word is tough. I'll say the sounds in (pause) **hot** the hard way. Listen. **H** (pause) **ooo** (pause) **t**.

e. Your turn. Say the sounds in (pause) **hot**. Get ready. Signal for each sound as the children say *h* (pause) *ooo* (pause) *t.* The children are to pause two seconds between the sounds. Repeat until firm.

f. Everybody, write the word (pause) **hot**. Check responses.

TASK 2 Children write hit, ham

a. You're going to write the word **hit**. Think about the sounds in (pause) **hit** and write the word. Check children's responses.

To correct	1. Say the sounds in **hit**. (Signal.) *Hiiit.*
	2. Say the sounds the hard way. (Signal.) *H* (pause) *iii* (pause) *t.*
	3. Write the word **hit**. Check children's responses.

b. Repeat *a* for **ham**.

TASK 3 Children write has

a. You're going to write the word (pause) **has**. Say the sounds you write for (pause) **has**. Get ready. Signal for each sound as the children say *h* (pause) *aaa* (pause) *sss.* The children are to pause two seconds between the sounds. Repeat until firm.

b. Everybody, write the word (pause) **has**. Check responses.

TASK 4 Children write sat, sit, not

a. You're going to write the word **sat**. Think about the sounds in (pause) **sat** and write the word. Check children's responses.

b. Repeat *a* for **sit** and **not**.

END OF SPELLING LESSON

Spelling Lesson 10

WORD WRITING

TASK 1 Children write at, is, on, not, if

a. You're going to write the word **at**. Think about the sounds in (pause) **at** and write the word. Check children's responses.

To correct	1. Say the sounds in **at**. (Signal.) *Aaat.*
	2. Say the sounds the hard way. (Signal.) *Aaa* (pause) *t.*
	3. Write the word **at**. Check children's responses.

b. You're going to write the word **is**. Think about the sounds in (pause) **is** and write the word. Check children's responses.

To correct	1. Say the sounds the hard way. (Signal.) *Iii* (pause) *sss.*
	2. Write the word **is**. Check children's responses.

c. Repeat *a* for **on**, **not**, and **if**.

TASK 2 Children write hot

a. You're going to write the word (pause) **hot**. This word is tough. I'll say the sounds in (pause) **hot** the hard way. Listen. H (pause) **ooo** (pause) t.

b. Your turn. Say the sounds in (pause) **hot**. Get ready. Signal for each sound as the children say *h* (pause) *ooo* (pause) *t*. The children are to pause two seconds between the sounds. Repeat until firm.

c. Everybody, write the word (pause) **hot**. Check children's responses.

TASK 3 Children write rim

a. You're going to write the word **rim**. Listen. **Rim**. Saying the sounds in (pause) **rim** the hard way. Get ready. Signal for each sound as the children say *rrr* (pause) *iii* (pause) *mmm*. The children are to pause two seconds between the sounds. Repeat until firm.

b. Everybody, write the word (pause) **rim**. Check children's responses.

TASK 4 Children write him

a. You're going to write the word (pause) **him**. This word is tough. I'll say the sounds in (pause) **him** the hard way. Listen. H (pause) **iii** (pause) **mmm**.

b. Your turn. Say the sounds in (pause) **him**. Get ready. Signal for each sound as the children say *h* (pause) *iii* (pause) *mmm*. The children are to pause two seconds between the sounds. Repeat until firm.

c. Everybody, write the word (pause) **him**. Check children's responses.

END OF SPELLING LESSON

Spelling Lesson 11

SOUND WRITING

TASK 1 Children write u

a. You're going to write a sound.

b. Here's the sound you're going to write. Listen. **uuu**. What sound? (Signal.) *uuu.*

c. Write **uuu**. Check children's responses.

WORD WRITING

TASK 2   Children write **sam, ham, not, hit, hat**

a. You're going to write the word **sam**. Think about the sounds in (pause) **sam** and write the word. Check children's responses.

To correct	**1.** Say the sounds in **sam**. (Signal.) *Sssaaammm.*
	2. Say the sounds the hard way. (Signal.) *Sss* (pause) *aaa* (pause) *mmm.*
	3. Write the word **sam**. Check children's responses.

b. Repeat *a* for the following: **ham, not, hit, hat.**

TASK 3   Children write **him**

a. You're going to write the word (pause) **him**. This word is tough. I'll say the sounds in (pause) **him** the hard way. Listen. **H** (pause) **iii** (pause) **mmm**.

b. Your turn. Say the sounds in (pause) **him**. Get ready. Signal for each sound as the children say *h* (pause) *iii* (pause) *mmm*. The children are to pause two seconds between the sounds. Repeat until firm.

c. Everybody, write the word (pause) **him**. Check children's responses.

TASK 4   Children write **on, if**

a. You're going to write the word **on**. Think about the sounds in (pause) **on** and write the word. Check children's responses.

b. Repeat *a* for **if.**

END OF SPELLING LESSON

Spelling Lesson 12

SOUND WRITING

TASK 1   Children write **u**

a. You're going to write a sound.

b. Here's the sound you're going to write. Listen. **uuu**.

What sound? (Signal.) *uuu.*

c. Write **uuu**. Check children's responses.

WORD WRITING

TASK 2   Children write **him**

a. You're going to write the word (pause) **him**. This word is tough. I'll say the sounds in (pause) **him** the hard way. Listen. **H** (pause) **iii** (pause) **mmm**.

b. Your turn. Say the sounds in (pause) **him**. Get ready. Signal for each sound as the children say *h* (pause) *iii* (pause) *mmm*. The children are to pause two seconds between the sounds. Repeat until firm.

c. Everybody, write the word (pause) **him**. Check children's responses.

TASK 3   Children write **sun**

a. You're going to write the word **sun**. Listen. **Sun**. Saying the sounds in (pause) **sun** the hard way. Get ready. Signal for each sound as the children say *sss* (pause) *uuu* (pause) *nnn*. The children are to pause two seconds between the sounds. Repeat until firm.

b. Everybody, write the word (pause) **sun**. Check children's responses.

TASK 4   Children write **not**

You're going to write the word **not**. Think about the sounds in (pause) **not** and write the word. Check children's responses.

To correct	1. Say the sounds in **not**. (Signal.) *Nnnooot.*
	2. Say the sounds the hard way. (Signal.) *Nnn* (pause) *ooo* (pause) *t.*
	3. Write the word **not**. Check children's responses.

TASK 5   Children write **nut**

a. You're going to write the word **nut**. Listen. **Nut**. Saying the sounds in (pause) **nut** the hard way. Get ready. Signal for each sound as the children say *nnn* (pause) *uuu* (pause) *t.* The children are to pause two seconds between the sounds. Repeat until firm.

b. Everybody, write the word (pause) **nut**. Check children's responses.

TASK 6   Children write **ron**

You're going to write the word **ron**. Think about the sounds in (pause) **ron** and write the word. Check children's responses.

TASK 7   Children write **run, fun**

a. You're going to write the word **run**. Listen. **Run**. Saying the sounds in (pause) **run** the hard way. Get ready. Signal for each sound as the children say *rrr* (pause) *uuu* (pause) *nnn.* The children are to pause two seconds between the sounds. Repeat until firm.

b. Everybody, write the word (pause) **run**. Check children's responses.

c. Repeat *a* and *b* for **fun.**

TASK 8   Children write **if**

You're going to write the word **if**. Think about the sounds in (pause) **if** and write the word. Check children's responses.

END OF SPELLING LESSON

Spelling Lesson 13

WORD WRITING

TASK 1   Children write **fun**

a. You're going to write the word **fun**. Listen. **Fun**. Saying the sounds in (pause) **fun** the hard way. Get ready. Signal for each sound as the children say *fff* (pause) *uuu* (pause) *nnn.* The children are to pause two seconds between the sounds. Repeat until firm.

b. Everybody, write the word (pause) **fun**. Check children's responses.

TASK 2   Children write **fin, on, am**

a. You're going to write the word **fin**. Think about the sounds in (pause) **fin** and write the word. Check children's responses.

To correct	1. Say the sounds in **fin**. (Signal.) *Fffiiinnn.*
	2. Say the sounds the hard way. (Signal.) *Fff* (pause) *iii* (pause) *nnn.*
	3. Write the word **fin**. Check children's responses.

b. Repeat *a* for **on** and **am.**

TASK 3   Children write **his**

a. You're going to write the word (pause) **his**. Say the sounds you write for (pause) **his**. Get ready. Signal for each sound as the children say *h* (pause) *iii* (pause) *sss.* The children are to pause two seconds between the sounds. Repeat until firm.

b. Everybody, write the word (pause) **his**. Check children's responses.

TASK 4   Children write **hot**

You're going to write the word **hot**. Think about the sounds in (pause) **hot** and write the word. Check children's responses.

TASK 5   Children write nut

a. You're going to write the word **nut**. Listen. **Nut**. Saying the sounds in (pause) **nut** the hard way. Get ready.   Signal for each sound as the children say *nnn* (pause) *uuu* (pause) *t.* The children are to pause two seconds between the sounds. Repeat until firm.

b. Everybody, write the word (pause) **nut**.   Check children's responses.

END OF SPELLING LESSON

Spelling Lesson 14

WORD WRITING

TASK 1   Children write ran

You're going to write the word **ran**. Think about the sounds in (pause) **ran** and write the word.   Check children's responses.

To correct	1. Say the sounds in **ran**. (Signal.) *Rrraaannn.*
	2. Say the sounds the hard way. (Signal.) *Rrr* (pause) *aaa* (pause) *nnn.*
	3. Write the word **ran**. Check children's responses.

TASK 2   Children write run

a. You're going to write the word **run**. Listen. **Run**. Saying the sounds in (pause) **run** the hard way. Get ready.   Signal for each sound as the children say *rrr* (pause) *uuu* (pause) *nnn.* The children are to pause two seconds between the sounds. Repeat until firm.

b. Everybody, write the word (pause) **run**.   Check children's responses.

TASK 3   Children write sit, sun, hot

a. You're going to write the word **sit**. Think about the sounds in (pause) **sit** and write the word.   Check children's responses.

b. Repeat *a* for **sun** and **hot**.

TASK 4   Children write hut

a. You're going to write the word **hut**. Listen. **Hut**. Saying the sounds in (pause) **hut** the hard way. Get ready.   Signal for each sound as the children say *h* (pause) *uuu* (pause) *t.* The children are to pause two seconds between the sounds. Repeat until firm.

b. Everybody, write the word (pause) **hut**.   Check children's responses.

TASK 5   Children write hit

You're going to write the word **hit**. Think about the sounds in (pause) **hit** and write the word.   Check children's responses.

END OF SPELLING LESSON

Spelling Lesson 15

WORD WRITING

TASK 1   Children write hum

a. You're going to write the word (pause) **hum**. This word is tough. I'll say the sounds in (pause) **hum** the hard way. Listen. **H** (pause) **uuu** (pause) **mmm**.

b. Your turn. Say the sounds in (pause) **hum**. Get ready.   Signal for each sound as the children say *h* (pause) *uuu* (pause) *mmm.* The children are to pause two seconds between the sounds. Repeat until firm.

c. Everybody, write the word (pause) **hum**.   Check children's responses.

TASK 2   Children write him, ham

a. You're going to write the word **him**. Think about the sounds in (pause) **him** and write the word.   Check children's responses.

To correct	1. Say the sounds in **him**. (Signal.) *Hiiimmm.*
	2. Say the sounds the hard way. (Signal.) *H* (pause) *iii* (pause) *mmm.*
	3. Write the word **him**. Check children's responses.

b. Repeat *a* for **ham**.

TASK 3   Children write **has**

a. You're going to write the word (pause) **has**. Say the sounds you write for (pause) **has**. Get ready. Signal for each sound as the children say *h* (pause) *aaa* (pause) *sss.* The children are to pause two seconds between the sounds. Repeat until firm.

b. Everybody, write the word (pause) **has**. Check children's responses.

TASK 4   Children write **not, nut, rut, on**

a. You're going to write the word **not**. Think about the sounds in (pause) **not** and write the word. Check children's responses.

b. Repeat *a* for **nut, rut,** and **on**.

END OF SPELLING LESSON

Spelling Lesson 16

WORD WRITING

TASK   Children write **fit, on, rat, his, has, mat, run, sit**

a. You're going to write the word **fit**. Think about the sounds in (pause) **fit** and write the word. Check children's responses.

To correct	1. Say the sounds in **fit**. (Signal.) *Fffiiit.*
	2. Say the sounds the hard way. (Signal.) *Fff* (pause) *iii* (pause) *t.*
	3. Write the word **fit**. Check children's responses.

b. Repeat *a* for **on** and **rat**.

c. You're going to write the word **his**. Think about the sounds in (pause) **his** and write the word. Check children's responses.

To correct	1. Say the sounds the hard way. (Signal.) *H* (pause) *iii* (pause) *sss.*
	2. Write the word **his**. Check children's responses.

d. Repeat *c* for **has**.

e. Repeat *a* for **mat, run,** and **sit**.

END OF SPELLING LESSON

Spelling Lesson 17

WORD WRITING

TASK   Children write **fat, run, is, fan, hut, hat, fun, hot**

a. You're going to write the word **fat**. Think about the sounds in (pause) **fat** and write the word. Check children's responses.

To correct	1. Say the sounds in **fat**. (Signal.) *Fffaaat.*
	2. Say the sounds the hard way. (Signal.) *Fff* (pause) *aaa* (pause) *t.*
	3. Write the word **fat**. Check children's responses.

b. Repeat *a* for **run**.

c. You're going to write the word **is**. Think about the sounds in (pause) **is** and write the word. Check children's responses.

To correct	1. Say the sounds the hard way. (Signal.) *Iii* (pause) *sss.*
	2. Write the word **is**. Check children's responses.

d. Repeat *a* for the following: **fan, hut, hat, fun, hot**.

END OF SPELLING LESSON

Spelling Lesson 18

WORD WRITING

TASK   Children write **fun, if, not, run, sit, ran, sat, fan**

a. You're going to write the word **fun**. Think about the sounds in (pause) **fun** and write the word. Check children's responses.

To correct	1. Say the sounds in **fun**. (Signal.) *Fffuuunnn.*
	2. Say the sounds the hard way. (Signal.) *Fff* (pause) *uuu* (pause) *nnn.*
	3. Write the word **fun**. Check children's responses.

b. Repeat *a* for the following: **if, not, run, sit, ran, sat, fan**.

END OF SPELLING LESSON

Spelling Lesson 19

WORD WRITING

TASK Children write **ham, nut, fat, hot, fun, hit, on, has**

a. You're going to write the word **ham**. Think about the sounds in (pause) **ham** and write the word. Check children's responses.

To correct	1. Say the sounds in **ham**. (Signal.) *Haaammm.*
	2. Say the sounds the hard way. (Signal.) *H* (pause) *aaa* (pause) *mmm.*
	3. Write the word **ham**. Check children's responses.

b. Repeat *a* for the following: **nut, fat, hot, fun, hit, on.**

c. You're going to write the word **has**. Think about the sounds in (pause) **has** and write the word. Check children's responses.

To correct	1. Say the sounds the hard way. (Signal.) *H* (pause) *aaa* (pause) *sss.*
	2. Write the word **has**. Check children's responses.

END OF SPELLING LESSON

Spelling Lesson 20

WORD WRITING

TASK Children write **rat, ran, fit, sun, rut, an, fin, hut**

a. You're going to write the word **rat**. Think about the sounds in (pause) **rat** and write the word. Check children's responses.

To correct	1. Say the sounds in **rat**. (Signal.) *Rrraaat.*
	2. Say the sounds the hard way. (Signal.) *Rrr* (pause) *aaa* (pause) *t.*
	3. Write the word **rat**. Check children's responses.

b. Repeat *a* for the following: **ran, fit, sun, rut, an, fin, hut.**

END OF SPELLING LESSON

Spelling Lesson 21

WORD WRITING

TASK Children write **him, ham, hot, if, am, hum, not, on**

a. You're going to write the word **him**. Think about the sounds in (pause) **him** and write the word. Check children's responses

To correct	1. Say the sounds in **him**. (Signal.) *Hiiimmm.*
	2. Say the sounds the hard way. (Signal.) *H* (pause) *iii* (pause) *mmn*
	3. Write the word **him**. Check children's responses.

b. Repeat *a* for the following: **ham, hot, if, am, hum, not, on.**

END OF SPELLING LESSON

Spelling Lesson 22

SOUND WRITING

TASK 1 Children write **d**

a. You're going to write a sound.

b. Here's the sound you're going to write. Listen. **d.** What sound? (Signal.) *d.*

c. Write **d**. Check children's responses.

WORD WRITING

TASK 2 Children write **is, an, run, mat, in, rut, on, hat**

a. You're going to write the word **is**. Think about the sounds in (pause) **is** and write the word. Check children's responses.

To correct	1. Say the sounds the hard way. (Signal.) *Iii* (pause) *sss.*
	2. Write the word **is**. Check children's responses.

TURN THE PAGE FOR THE REST OF TASK 2.

b. You're going to write the word **an**. Think about the sounds in (pause) **an** and write the word. Check children's responses.

To correct	1. Say the sounds in **an**. (Signal.) *Aaannn*.
	2. Say the sounds the hard way. (Signal.) *Aaa* (pause) *nnn*.
	3. Write the word **an**. Check children's responses.

c. Repeat *b* for the following: **run, mat, in, rut, on, hat.**

END OF SPELLING LESSON

Spelling Lesson 23

SOUND WRITING

TASK 1   Children write **d**

a. You're going to write a sound.

b. Here's the sound you're going to write. Listen. **d**.
What sound? (Signal.) *d*.

c. Write **d**. Check children's responses.

WORD WRITING

TASK 2   Children write **has, mat**

a. You're going to write the word **has**. Think about the sounds in (pause) **has** and write the word. Check children's responses.

| To correct | 1. Say the sounds the hard way. (Signal.) *H* (pause) *aaa* (pause) *sss*. |
| | 2. Write the word **has**. Check children's responses. |

b. Now you're going to write the word **mat**. Think about the sounds in (pause) **mat** and write the word. Check children's responses.

To correct	1. Say the sounds in **mat**. (Signal.) *Mmmaaat*.
	2. Say the sounds the hard way. (Signal.) *Mmm* (pause) *aaa* (pause) *t*.
	3. Write the word **mat**. Check children's responses.

TASK 3   Children write **mad**

a. You're going to write the word **mad**. Listen. **Mad**. Saying the sounds in (pause) **mad** the hard way. Get ready. Signal for each sound as the children say *mmm* (pause) *aaa* (pause) *d*. The children are to pause two seconds between the sounds. Repeat until firm.

b. Everybody, write the word (pause) **mad** Check responses.

TASK 4   Children write **if**

You're going to write the word **if**. Think about the sounds in (pause) **if** and write the word. Check children's responses.

TASK 5   Children write **sad**

a. You're going to write the word **sad**. Listen. **Sad**. Saying the sounds in (pause) **sad** the hard way. Get ready. Signal for each sound as the children say *sss* (pause) *aaa* (pause) *d*. The children are to pause two seconds between the sounds. Repeat until firm.

b. Everybody, write the word (pause) **sad**. Check responses.

TASK 6   Children write **had**

a. You're going to write the word (pause) **had**. This word is tough. I'll say the sounds in (pause) **had** the hard way. Listen. **H** (pause one second) *aaa* (pause one second) **d**.

b. Your turn. Say the sounds in (pause) **had**. Get ready. Signal for each sound as the children say *h* (pause) *aaa* (pause) *d*. The children are to pause two seconds between the sounds. Repeat until firm.

c. Everybody, write the word (pause) **had**. Check children's responses.

TASK 7   Children write **hot, nut**

a. You're going to write the word **hot**. Think about the sounds in (pause) **hot** and write the word. Check children's responses.

b. Repeat *a* for **nut**.

END OF SPELLING LESSON

Spelling Lesson 24

WORD WRITING

TASK 1   Children write **mad, mud, sad**

a. You're going to write the word **mad**. Listen. **Mad**. Saying the sounds in (pause) **mad** the hard way. Get ready. Signal for each sound as the children say *mmm* (pause) *aaa* (pause) *d*. The children are to pause two seconds between the sounds. Repeat until firm.

b. Everybody, write the word (pause) **mad**. Check children's responses.

c. Repeat *a* and *b* for **mud** and **sad**.

TASK 2   Children write **mat, on**

a. You're going to write the word **mat**. Think about the sounds in (pause) **mat** and write the word. Check children's responses.

To correct	1. Say the sounds in **mat**. (Signal.) *Mmmaaat.*
	2. Say the sounds the hard way. (Signal.) *Mmm (pause) aaa (pause) t.*
	3. Write the word **mat**. Check children's responses.

b. Repeat *a* for **on**.

TASK 3   Children write **had**

a. You're going to write the word (pause) **had**. This word is tough. I'll say the sounds in (pause) **had** the hard way. Listen. **H** (pause one second) **aaa** (pause one second) **d**.

b. Your turn. Say the sounds in (pause) **had**. Get ready. Signal for each sound as the children say *h* (pause) *aaa* (pause) *d*. The children are to pause two seconds between the sounds. Repeat until firm.

c. Everybody, write the word (pause) **had**. Check children's responses.

TASK 4   Children write **sit**

You're going to write the word **sit**. Think about the sounds in (pause) **sit** and write the word. Check children's responses.

END OF SPELLING LESSON

Spelling Lesson 25

WORD WRITING

TASK 1   Children write **hot, sad**

a. You're going to write the word **hot**. Think about the sounds in (pause) **hot** and write the word. Check children's responses.

To correct	1. Say the sounds in **hot**. (Signal.) *Hooot.*
	2. Say the sounds the hard way. (Signal.) *H (pause) ooo (pause) t.*
	3. Write the word **hot**. Check children's responses.

b. Repeat *a* for **sad**.

TASK 2   Children write **nod**

a. You're going to write the word **nod**. Listen. **Nod**. Saying the sounds in (pause) **nod** the hard way. Get ready. Signal for each sound as the children say *nnn* (pause) *ooo* (pause) *d*. The children are to pause two seconds between the sounds. Repeat until firm.

b. Everybody, write the word (pause) **nod**. Check children's responses.

TASK 3   Children write **hum, his, him, nut, has**

a. You're going to write the word **hum**. Think about the sounds in (pause) **hum** and write the word. Check children's responses.

b. You're going to write the word **his**. Think about the sounds in (pause) **his** and write the word. Check children's responses.

| To correct | 1. Say the sounds the hard way. (Signal.) *H (pause) iii (pause) sss.* |
| | 2. Write the word **his**. Check children's responses. |

c. Repeat *a* for **him** and **nut**.

d. Repeat *b* for **has**.

END OF SPELLING LESSON

Spelling Lesson 26

WORD WRITING

TASK 1 Children write **sad, sun**

a. You're going to write the word **sad**. Think about the sounds in (pause) **sad** and write the word. Check children's responses.

To correct	1. Say the sounds in **sad**. (Signal.) *Sssaaad.*
	2. Say the sounds the hard way. (Signal.) *Sss* (pause) *aaa* (pause) *d.*
	3. Write the word **sad**. Check children's responses.

b. Repeat *a* for **sun.**

TASK 2 Children write **rid**

a. You're going to write the word **rid**. Listen. **Rid**. Saying the sounds in (pause) **rid** the hard way. Get ready. Signal for each sound as the children say *rrr* (pause) *iii* (pause) *d*. The children are to pause two seconds between the sounds. Repeat until firm.

b. Everybody, write the word (pause) **rid**. Check children's responses.

TASK 3 Children write **run, mad, it, mud, sit**

a. You're going to write the word **run**. Think about the sounds in (pause) **run** and write the word. Check children's responses.

b. Repeat *a* for the following: **mad, it, mud, sit.**

END OF SPELLING LESSON

Spelling Lesson 27

WORD WRITING

TASK 1 Children write **an, ran**

a. You're going to write the word **an**. Think about the sounds in (pause) **an** and write the word. Check children's responses.

To correct	1. Say the sounds in **an**. (Signal.) *Aaannn.*
	2. Say the sounds the hard way. (Signal.) *Aaa* (pause) *nnn.*
	3. Write the word **an**. Check children's responses.

b. Repeat *a* for **ran.**

TASK 2 Children write **dan, tan**

a. You're going to write the word (pause) **dan**. This word is tough. I'll say the sounds in (pause) **dan** the hard way. Listen. **D** (pause) **aaa** (pause) **nnn.**

b. Your turn. Say the sounds in (pause) **dan**. Get ready. Signal for each sound as the children say *d* (pause) *aaa* (pause) *nnn*. The children are to pause two seconds between sounds. Repeat until firm.

c. Everybody, write the word (pause) **dan**. Check children's responses.

d. Now you're going to write the word (pause) **tan**. This word is tough. I'll say the sounds in (pause) **tan** the hard way. Listen. **T** (pause) **aaa** (pause) **nnn.**

e. Your turn. Say the sounds in (pause) **tan**. Get ready. Signal for each sound as the children say *t* (pause) *aaa* (pause) *nnn*. The children are to pause two seconds between sounds. Repeat until firm.

f. Everybody, write the word (pause) **tan**. Check children's responses.

TASK 3 Children write **sun, fin, nut, mud**

a. You're going to write the word **sun**. Think about the sounds in (pause) **sun** and write the word. Check children's responses.

b. Repeat *a* for **fin, nut,** and **mud.**

END OF SPELLING LESSON

Spelling Lesson 28

WORD WRITING

TASK 1 Children write **mud**

You're going to write the word **mud**. Think about the sounds in (pause) **mud** and write the word. Check children's responses.

To correct	1. Say the sounds in **mud**. (Signal.) *Mmmuuud*. 2. Say the sounds the hard way. (Signal.) *Mmm* (pause) *uuu* (pause) *d*. 3. Write the word **mud**. Check children's responses.

TASK 2 Children write **tan**

a. You're going to write the word (pause) **tan**. This word is tough. I'll say the sounds in (pause) **tan** the hard way. Listen. *T* (pause) *aaa* (pause) *nnn*.

b. Your turn. Say the sounds in (pause) **tan**. Get ready. Signal for each sound as the children say *t* (pause) *aaa* (pause) *nnn*. The children are to pause two seconds between sounds. Repeat until firm.

c. Everybody, write the word (pause) **tan**. Check children's responses.

TASK 3 Children write **not, fin, hat, fat, his, him**

a. You're going to write the word **not**. Think about the sounds in (pause) **not** and write the word. Check children's responses.

b. Repeat a for **fin, hat**, and **fat**.

c. You're going to write the word **his**. Think about the sounds in (pause) **his** and write the word. Check children's responses.

To correct	1. Say the sounds the hard way. (Signal.) *H* (pause) *iii* (pause) *sss*. 2. Write the word **his**. Check children's responses.

d. Repeat a for **him**.

Spelling Lesson 29

SOUND WRITING

TASK 1 Children write $\bar{e}$

a. You're going to write a sound.

b. Here's the sound you're going to write. Listen. $\bar{e}\bar{e}\bar{e}$. What sound? (Signal.) $\bar{e}\bar{e}\bar{e}$.

c. Write $\bar{e}\bar{e}\bar{e}$. Check children's responses.

WORD WRITING

TASK 2 Children write **ron, an**

a. You're going to write the word **ron**. Think about the sounds in (pause) **ron** and write the word. Check children's responses.

To correct	1. Say the sounds in **ron**. (Signal.) *Rrrooonnn*. 2. Say the sounds the hard way. (Signal.) *Rrr* (pause) *ooo* (pause) *nnn*. 3. Write the word **ron**. Check children's responses.

b. Repeat a for **an**.

TASK 3 Children write **and**

a. You're going to write the word **and**. Listen. **And**. Saying the sounds in (pause) **and** the hard way. Get ready. Signal for each sound as the children say *aaa* (pause) *nnn* (pause) *d*. The children are to pause two seconds between the sounds. Repeat until firm.

b. Everybody, write the word (pause) **and**. Check children's responses.

TASK 4 Children write **hit**

You're going to write the word **hit**. Think about the sounds in (pause) **hit** and write the word. Check children's responses.

END OF SPELLING LESSON

TASK 5   Children write tan

a. You're going to write the word (pause) tan. This word is tough. I'll say the sounds in (pause) tan the hard way. Listen. T (pause) aaa (pause) nnn.

b. Your turn. Say the sounds in (pause) tan. Get ready. Signal for each sound as the children say *t* (pause) *aaa* (pause) *nnn*. The children are to pause two seconds between the sounds. Repeat until firm.

c. Everybody, write the word (pause) tan. Check responses.

TASK 6   Children write sit, his

a. You're going to write the word sit. Think about the sounds in (pause) sit and write the word. Check children's responses.

b. Repeat *a* for his.

END OF SPELLING LESSON

Spelling Lesson 30

SOUND WRITING

TASK 1   Children write $\bar{e}$

a. You're going to write a sound.

b. Here's the sound you're going to write. Listen. $\overline{eee}$. What sound? (Signal.) $\overline{eee}$.

c. Write $\overline{eee}$. Check children's responses.

WORD WRITING

TASK 2   Children write me

a. You're going to write the word me. Listen. Me. Saying the sounds in (pause) me the hard way. Get ready. Signal for each sound as the children say *mmm* (pause) $\overline{eee}$. The children are to pause two seconds between the sounds. Repeat until firm.

b. Everybody, write the word (pause) me. Check children's responses.

TASK 3   Children write he

a. You're going to write the word (pause) he. This word is tough. I'll say the sounds in (pause) he the hard way. Listen. H (pause one second) $\overline{eee}$.

b. Your turn. Say the sounds in (pause) he. Get ready. Signal for each sound as the children say *h* (pause) $\overline{eee}$. The children are to pause two seconds between the sounds. Repeat until firm.

c. Everybody, write the word (pause) he. Check responses.

TASK 4   Children write ham

You're going to write the word ham. Think about the sounds in (pause) ham and write the word. Check children's responses.

TASK 5   Children write and

a. You're going to write the word and. Listen. And. Saying the sounds in (pause) and the hard way. Get ready. Signal for each sound as the children say *aaa* (pause) *nnn* (pause) *d*. The children are to pause two seconds between the sounds. Repeat until firm.

b. Everybody, write the word (pause) and. Check responses.

TASK 6   Children write hand

a. You're going to write the word (pause) hand. This word is tough. I'll say the sounds in (pause) hand the hard way. Listen. H (pause) aaa (pause) nnn (pause) d.

b. Your turn. Say the sounds in (pause) hand. Get ready. Signal for each sound as the children say *h* (pause) *aaa* (pause) *nnn* (pause) *d*. The children are to pause two seconds between sounds. Repeat until firm.

c. Everybody, write the word (pause) hand. Check responses.

TASK 7   Children write mud, fit

a. You're going to write the word mud. Think about the sounds in (pause) mud and write the word. Check children's responses.

b. Repeat *a* for fit.

END OF SPELLING LESSON

Spelling Lesson 31

WORD WRITING

TASK 1 Children write **me**

a. You're going to write the word **me**. Listen. **Me**. Saying the sounds in (pause) **me** the hard way. Get ready. Signal for each sound as the children say *mmm* (pause) *ēēē*. The children are to pause two seconds between the sounds. Repeat until firm.

b. Everybody, write the word (pause) **me**. Check responses.

TASK 2 Children write **he**

a. You're going to write the word (pause) **he**. This word is tough. I'll say the sounds in (pause) **he** the hard way. Listen. **H** (pause one second) *ēēē*.

b. Your turn. Say the sounds in (pause) **he**. Get ready. Signal for each sound as the children say *h* (pause) *eee.* The children are to pause two seconds between the sounds. Repeat until firm.

c. Everybody, write the word (pause) **he**. Check children's responses.

TASK 3 Children write **tan, fit**

a. You're going to write the word **tan**. Think about the sounds in (pause) **tan** and write the word. Check children's responses.

To correct	1. Say the sounds in **tan**. (Signal.) *Taaannn.*
	2. Say the sounds the hard way. (Signal.) *T* (pause) *aaa* (pause) *nnn*.
	3. Write the word **tan**. Check children's responses.

b. Repeat *a* for **fit**.

TASK 4 Children write **and**

a. You're going to write the word **and**. Listen. **And**. Saying the sounds in (pause) **and** the hard way. Get ready. Signal for each sound as the children say *aaa* (pause) *nnn* (pause) *d*. The children are to pause two seconds between the sounds. Repeat until firm.

b. Everybody, write the word (pause) **and**. Check responses.

TASK 5 Children write **hand**

a. You're going to write the word (pause) **hand**. This word is tough. I'll say the sounds in (pause) **hand** the hard way. Listen. **H** (pause) **aaa** (pause) **nnn** (pause) **d**.

b. Your turn. Say the sounds in (pause) **hand**. Get ready. Signal for each sound as the children say *h* (pause) *aaa* (pause) *nnn* (pause) *d*. The children are to pause two seconds between the sounds. Repeat until firm.

c. Everybody, write the word (pause) **hand**. Check responses.

TASK 6 Children write **fan, sin**

a. You're going to write the word **fan**. Think about the sounds in (pause) **fan** and write the word. Check children's responses.

b. Repeat *a* for **sin**.

END OF SPELLING LESSON

Spelling Lesson 32

SOUND WRITING

TASK 1 Children write **w**

a. You're going to write a sound.

b. Here's the sound you're going to write. Listen. **www**. What sound? (Signal.) *www.*

c. Write **www**. Check children's responses.

WORD WRITING

TASK 2 Children write **he**

a. You're going to write the word **he**. Listen. **He**. Saying the sounds in (pause) **he** the hard way. Get ready. Signal for each sound as the children say *h* (pause) *ēēē*. The children are to pause two seconds between the sounds. Repeat until firm.

b. Everybody, write the word (pause) **he**. Check children's responses.

TASK 3 Children write **hand**

a. You're going to write the word (pause) **hand**. This word is tough.
I'll say the sounds in (pause) **hand** the hard way. Listen.
H (pause) **aaa** (pause) **nnn** (pause) **d**.

b. Your turn. Say the sounds in (pause) **hand**. Get ready.
Signal for each sound as the children say *h* (pause) *aaa* (pause)
nnn (pause) *d*. The children are to pause two seconds between the
sounds. Repeat until firm.

c. Everybody, write the word (pause) **hand**. Check children's
responses.

TASK 4 Children write **me**

a. You're going to write the word **me**. Listen. **Me**. Saying the sounds
in (pause) **me** the hard way. Get ready. Signal for each sound
as the children say *mmm* (pause) *ēēē*. The children are to pause
two seconds between the sounds. Repeat until firm.

b. Everybody, write the word (pause) **me**. Check children's
responses.

TASK 5 Children write **tan, dan, in**

a. You're going to write the word **tan**. Think about the sounds in
tan and write the word. Check children's responses.

To correct	1. Say the sounds in **tan**. (Signal.) *Taaannn.*
	2. Say the sounds the hard way. (Signal.) *T* (pause) *aaa* (pause) *nnn*.
	3. Write the word **tan**. Check children's responses.

b. Repeat *a* for **dan** and **in**.

TASK 6 Children write **tin**

a. You're going to write the word (pause) **tin**. This word is tough.
I'll say the sounds in (pause) **tin** the hard way. Listen.
T (pause) **iii** (pause) **nnn**.

b. Your turn. Say the sounds in (pause) **tin**. Get ready.
Signal for each sound as the children say *t* (pause) *iii* (pause) *nnn*.
The children are to pause two seconds between the sounds.
Repeat until firm.

c. Everybody, write the word (pause) **tin**. Check children's responses.

22

TASK 7 Children write **has**

You're going to write the word **has**. Think about the sounds in (pause)
has and write the word. Check children's responses.

| To correct | 1. Say the sounds the hard way. (Signal.) *H* (pause) *aaa* (pause) *sss*. |
| | 2. Write the word **has**. Check children's responses. |

END OF SPELLING LESSON

Spelling Lesson 33

SOUND WRITING

TASK 1 Children write **w**

a. You're going to write a sound.
b. Here's the sound you're going to write. Listen. **www**. What sound?
(Signal.) *www.*

c. Write **www**. Check children's responses.

WORD WRITING

TASK 2 Children write **we, had**

a. You're going to write the word **we**. Listen. **We**. Saying the sounds
in (pause) **we** the hard way. Get ready. Signal for each sound
as the children say *www* (pause) *ēēē*. The children are to pause
two seconds between the sounds. Repeat until firm.

b. Everybody, write the word (pause) **we**. Check children's
responses.

c. Repeat *a* and *b* for **had**.

TASK 3   Children write **he**

You're going to write the word **he**. Think about the sounds in (pause) **he** and write the word. Check children's responses.

To correct	1. Say the sounds in **he**. (Signal.) *Hēēē*.
	2. Say the sounds the hard way. (Signal.) *H* (pause) *ēēē*.
	3. Write the word **he**. Check children's responses.

TASK 4   Children write **win**

a. You're going to write the word **win**. Listen. **Win**. Saying the sounds in (pause) **win** the hard way. Get ready. Signal for each sound as the children say *www* (pause) *iii* (pause) *nnn*. The children are to pause two seconds between the sounds. Repeat until firm.

b. Everybody, write the word (pause) **win**. Check children's responses.

TASK 5   Children write **fit**, **if**, **on**

a. You're going to write the word **fit**. Think about the sounds in (pause) **fit** and write the word. Check children's responses.

b. Repeat *a* for **if** and **on**.

END OF SPELLING LESSON

Spelling Lesson 34

WORD WRITING

TASK 1   Children write **dan**, **on**

a. You're going to write the word **dan**. Think about the sounds in (pause) **dan** and write the word. Check children's responses.

To correct	1. Say the sounds in **dan**. (Signal.) *Daaannn*.
	2. Say the sounds the hard way. (Signal.) *D* (pause) *aaa* (pause) *nnn*.
	3. Write the word **dan**. Check children's responses.

b. Repeat *a* for **on**.

TASK 2   Children write **we**

a. You're going to write the word **we**. Listen. **We**. Saying the sounds in (pause) **we** the hard way. Get ready. Signal for each sound as the children say *www* (pause) *ēēē*. The children are to pause two seconds between the sounds. Repeat until firm.

b. Everybody, write the word (pause) **we**. Check children's responses.

TASK 3   Children write **in**, **sun**, **he**, **it**, **at**

a. You're going to write the word **in**. Think about the sounds in (pause) **in** and write the word. Check children's responses.

b. Repeat *a* for the following: **sun**, **he**, **it**, **at**.

END OF SPELLING LESSON

Spelling Lesson 35

WORD WRITING

TASK   Children write **we**, **an**, **at**, **if**, **is**, **and**, **has**, **his**

a. You're going to write the word **we**. Think about the sounds in (pause) **we** and write the word. Check children's responses.

To correct	1. Say the sounds in **we**. (Signal.) *Wwwēēē*.
	2. Say the sounds the hard way. (Signal.) *Www* (pause) *ēēē*.
	3. Write the word **we**. Check children's responses.

b. Repeat *a* for **an**, **at**, and **if**.

c. You're going to write the word **is**. Think about the sounds in (pause) **is** and write the word. Check children's responses.

| To correct | 1. Say the sounds the hard way. (Signal.) *Iii* (pause) *sss*. |
| | 2. Write the word **is**. Check children's responses. |

d. Repeat *a* for **and**.

e. Repeat *c* for **has** and **his**.

END OF SPELLING LESSON

Spelling Lesson 36

SOUND WRITING

TASK 1   Children write I as in land

a You're going to write a sound.

b Here's the sound you're going to write. Listen. **lll.**

What sound? (Signal.) *lll.*

c. Write **lll.** Check children's responses.

WORD WRITING

TASK 2   Children write he, tan, mad, we

a. You're going to write the word **he.** Think about the sounds in (pause) **he** and write the word. Check children's responses.

To correct	1. Say the sounds in **he.** (Signal.) *Hēēē.*
	2. Say the sounds the hard way. (Signal.) *H* (pause) *ēēē.*
	3. Write the word **he.** Check children's responses.

b. Repeat *a* for **tan, mad** and **we.**

TASK 3   Children write land

a. You're going to write the word **land.** Listen. **Land.** Saying the sounds in (pause) **land** the hard way. Get ready. Signal for each sound as the children say *lll* (pause) *aaa* (pause) *nnn* (pause) *d.* The children are to pause two seconds between the sounds. Repeat until firm.

b. Everybody, write the word (pause) **land.** Check children's responses.

TASK 4   Children write has, mud

a. You're going to write the word **has.** Think about the sounds in (pause) **has** and write the word. Check children's responses.

To correct	1. Say the sounds the hard way. (Signal.) *H* (pause) *aaa* (pause) *sss.*
	2. Write the word **has.** Check children's responses.

b. Repeat *a* for **mud.**

END OF SPELLING LESSON

Spelling Lesson 37

SOUND WRITING

TASK 1   Children write I as in land

a You're going to write a sound.

b Here's the sound you're going to write. Listen. **lll.**

What sound? (Signal.) *lll.*

c Write **lll.** Check children's responses.

WORD WRITING

TASK 2   Children write nod

a You're going to write the word **nod.** Listen. **Nod.** Saying the sounds in (pause) **nod** the hard way. Get ready. Signal for each sound as the children say *nnn* (pause) *ooo* (pause) *d.* The children are to pause two seconds between the sounds. Repeat until firm.

b. Everybody, write the word (pause) **nod.** Check children's responses.

TASK 3 Children write and, hand, land

a. You're going to write the word **and**. Think about the sounds in (pause) **and** and write the word. Check children's responses.

To correct	1. Say the sounds in **and**. (Signal.) *Aaannnd*.
	2. Say the sounds the hard way. (Signal.) *Aaa* (pause) *nnn* (pause) *d*.
	3. Write the word **and**. Check children's responses.

b. Repeat *a* for **hand** and **land**.

TASK 4 Children write rid, lid

a. You're going to write the word **rid**. Listen. **Rid**. Saying the sounds in (pause) **rid** the hard way. Get ready. Signal for each sound as the children say *rrr* (pause) *iii* (pause) *d.* The children are to pause two seconds between the sounds. Repeat until firm.

b. Everybody, write the word (pause) **rid**. Check children's responses.

c. Repeat *a* and *b* for **lid**.

TASK 5 Children write if

You're going to write the word **if**. Think about the sounds in (pause) **if** and write the word. Check children's responses.

END OF SPELLING LESSON

Spelling Lesson 38

WORD WRITING

TASK 1 Children write hand, we, land, me, has

a. You're going to write the word **hand**. Think about the sounds in (pause) **hand** and write the word. Check children's responses.

b. Repeat *a* for **we, land,** and **me**.

c. You're going to write the word **has**. Think about the sounds in (pause) **has** and write the word. Check children's responses.

| To correct | 1. Say the sounds the hard way. (Signal.) *H* (pause) *aaa* (pause) *sss*. |
| | 2. Write the word **has**. Check children's responses. |

TASK 2 Children write win

a. You're going to write the word **win**. Listen. **Win**. Saying the sounds in (pause) **win** the hard way. Get ready. Signal for each sound as the children say *www* (pause) *iii* (pause) *nnn*. The children are to pause two seconds between the sounds. Repeat until firm.

b. Everybody, write the word (pause) **win**. Check children's responses.

TASK 3 Children write sit, lit

a. You're going to write the word **sit**. Think about the sounds in (pause) **sit** and write the word. Check children's responses.

b. Repeat *a* for **lit**.

END OF SPELLING LESSON

Spelling Lesson 39

WORD WRITING

TASK Children write hot, hand, mud, tan, dan, nut, if, land

a. You're going to write the word **hot**. Think about the sounds in (pause) **hot** and write the word. Check children's responses.

To correct	1. Say the sounds in **hot**. (Signal.) *Hooot*.
	2. Say the sounds the hard way. (Signal.) *H* (pause) *ooo* (pause) *t*.
	3. Write the word **hot**. Check children's responses.

b. Repeat *a* for the following: **hand, mud, tan, dan, nut, if, land.**

END OF SPELLING LESSON

Spelling Lesson 40

WORD WRITING

TASK   Children write **nod, fit, tan, dan, fin, tin, his**

a. You're going to write the word **nod**. Think about the sounds in (pause) **nod** and write the word. Check children's responses.

To correct	1. Say the sounds in **nod**. (Signal.) *Nnnoood.* 2. Say the sounds the hard way. (Signal.) *Nnn* (pause) *ooo* (pause) *d.* 3. Write the word **nod**. Check children's responses.

b. Repeat *a* for the following: **fit, tan, dan, fin, tin.**

c. You're going to write the word **his**. Think about the sounds in (pause) **his** and write the word. Check children's responses.

To correct	1. Say the sounds the hard way. (Signal.) *H* (pause) *iii* (pause) *sss.* 2. Write the word **his**. Check children's responses.

END OF SPELLING LESSON

Spelling Lesson 41

WORD WRITING

TASK 1   Children write **did, rid, hid**

a. You're going to write the word **did**. Listen. **Did**. Saying the sounds in (pause) **did** the hard way. Get ready. Signal for each sound as the children say *d* (pause) *iii* (pause) *d.* The children are to pause two seconds between the sounds. Repeat until firm.

b. Everybody, write the word (pause) **did**. Check children's responses.

c. Repeat *a* and *b* for **rid** and **hid**.

TASK 2   Children write **sin, tin, hand**

a. You're going to write the word **sin**. Think about the sounds in (pause) **sin** and write the word. Check children's responses.

To correct	1. Say the sounds in **sin**. (Signal.) *Sssiiinnn.* 2. Say the sounds the hard way. (Signal.) *Sss* (pause) *iii* (pause) *nnn.* 3. Write the word **sin**. Check children's responses.

b. Repeat *a* for **tin** and **hand.**

TASK 3   Children write **sand**

a. You're going to write the word **sand**. Listen. **Sand**. Saying the sounds in (pause) **sand** the hard way. Get ready. Signal for each sound as the children say *sss* (pause) *aaa* (pause) *nnn* (pause) *d.* The children are to pause two seconds between the sounds. Repeat until firm.

b. Everybody, write the word (pause) **sand**. Check children's responses.

END OF SPELLING LESSON

Spelling Lesson 42

WORD WRITING

TASK 1   Children write **did, dad**

a. You're going to write **did**. Listen. **Did**. Saying the sounds in (pause) **did** the hard way. Get ready. Signal for each sound as the children say *d* (pause) *iii* (pause) *d.* The children are to pause two seconds between the sounds. Repeat until firm.

b. Everybody, write the word (pause) **did**. Check children's responses.

c. Repeat *a* and *b* for **dad.**

TASK 2 Children write **tin**

You're going to write the word **tin**. Think about the sounds in (pause) **tin** and write the word. Check children's responses.

To correct	1. Say the sounds in **tin**. (Signal.) *Tiiinnn.* 2. Say the sounds the hard way. (Signal.) *T* (pause) *iii* (pause) *nnn.* 3. Write the word **tin**. Check children's responses.

TASK 3 Children write **sand**

a. You're going to write the word **sand**. Listen. **Sand**. Saying the sounds in (pause) **sand** the hard way. Get ready. Signal for each sound as the children say *sss* (pause) *aaa* (pause) *nnn* (pause) *d.* The children are to pause two seconds between the sounds. Repeat until firm.

b. Everybody, write the word (pause) **sand**. Check children's responses.

TASK 4 Children write **not, me, his**

a. You're going to write the word **not**. Think about the sounds in (pause) **not** and write the word. Check children's responses.

To correct	1. Say the sounds in **not**. (Signal.) *Nnnooot.* 2. Say the sounds the hard way. (Signal.) *Nnn* (pause) *ooo* (pause) *t.* 3. Write the word **not**. Check children's responses.

b. Repeat *a* for **me**.

c. You're going to write the word **his**. Think about the sounds in (pause) **his** and write the word. Check children's responses.

To correct	1. Say the sounds the hard way. (Signal.) *H* (pause) *iii* (pause) *sss.* 2. Write the word **his**. Check children's responses.

END OF SPELLING LESSON

Spelling Lesson 43

WORD WRITING

TASK 1 Children write **sun, sit, he, sad**

a. You're going to write the word **sun**. Think about the sounds in (pause) **sun** and write the word. Check children's responses.

To correct	1. Say the sounds in **sun**. (Signal.) *Sssuuunnn.* 2. Say the sounds the hard way. (Signal.) *Sss* (pause) *uuu* (pause) *nnn.* 3. Write the word **sun**. Check children's responses.

b. Repeat *a* for **sit, he,** and **sad**.

TASK 2 Children write **dad**

a. You're going to write the word **dad**. Listen. **Dad**. Saying the sounds in (pause) **dad** the hard way. Get ready. Signal for each sound as the children say *d* (pause) *aaa* (pause) *d.* The children are to pause two seconds between the sounds. Repeat until firm.

b. Everybody, write the word (pause) **dad**. Check children's responses.

TASK 3 Children write **had, ron, fit**

a. You're going to write the word **had**. Think about the sounds in (pause) **had** and write the word. Check children's responses.

b. Repeat *a* for **ron** and **fit**.

END OF SPELLING LESSON

Spelling Lesson 44

WORD WRITING

TASK 1   Children write **did**

a. You're going to write the word **did**. Listen. **Did**. Saying the sounds in (pause) **did** the hard way. Get ready.   Signal for each sound as the children say *d* (pause) *iii* (pause) *d.* The children are to pause two seconds between the sounds. Repeat until firm.

b. Everybody, write the word (pause) **did**.   Check children's responses.

TASK 2   Children write **land**, **not**

a. You're going to write the word **land**. Think about the sounds in (pause) **land** and write the word.   Check children's responses.

To correct	1. Say the sounds in **land**. (Signal.) *Lllaaannnd.* 2. Say the sounds the hard way. (Signal.) *Lll* (pause) *aaa* (pause) *nnn* (pause) *d.* 3. Write the word **land**. Check children's responses.

b. Repeat *a* for **not**.

TASK 3   Children write **hid**

a. You're going to write the word **hid**. Listen. **Hid**. Saying the sounds in (pause) **hid** the hard way. Get ready.   Signal for each sound as the children say *h* (pause) *iii* (pause) *d.* The children are to pause two seconds between the sounds. Repeat until firm.

b. Everybody, write the word (pause) **hid**.   Check children's responses.

TASK 4   Children write **has**, **mud**, **hot**, **we**

a. You're going to write the word **has**. Think about the sounds in (pause) **has** and write the word.   Check children's responses.

To correct	1. Say the sounds the hard way. (Signal.) *H* (pause) *aaa* (pause) *sss.* 2. Write the word **has**. Check children's responses.

b. You're going to write the word **mud**. Think about the sounds in (pause) **mud** and write the word.   Check children's responses.

To correct	1. Say the sounds in **mud**. (Signal.) *Mmmuuud.* 2. Say the sounds the hard way. (Signal.) *Mmm* (pause) *uuu* (pause) *d.* 3. Write the word **mud**. Check children's responses.

c. Repeat *b* for **hot** and **we**.

END OF SPELLING LESSON

Spelling Lesson 45

WORD WRITING

TASK   Children write **and**, **land**, **sand**, **hand**, **if**, **has**, **is**, **on**

a. You're going to write the word **and**. Think about the sounds in (pause) **and** and write the word.   Check children's responses.

To correct	1. Say the sounds in **and**. (Signal.) *Aaannnd.* 2. Say the sounds the hard way. (Signal.) *Aaa* (pause) *nnn* (pause) *d.* 3. Write the word **and**. Check children's responses.

b. Repeat *a* for the following: **land, sand, hand, if.**

c. You're going to write the word **has**. Think about the sounds in (pause) **has** and write the word.   Check children's responses.

To correct	1. Say the sounds the hard way. (Signal.) *H* (pause) *aaa* (pause) *sss.* 2. Write the word **has**. Check children's responses.

d. Repeat *c* for **is**.

e. Repeat *a* for **on**.

END OF SPELLING LESSON

Spelling Lesson 46

WORD WRITING

TASK 1   Children write **me**

You're going to write the word **me**. Think about the sounds in
(pause) **me** and write the word. Check children's responses.

To correct	1. Say the sounds in **me**. (Signal.) *Mmmēēē.*
	2. Say the sounds the hard way. (Signal.) *Mmm*
	(pause) *ēēē.*
	3. Write the word **me**. Check children's responses.

TASK 2   Children write **win**

a. You're going to write the word **win**. Listen. **Win.** Saying the sounds
   in (pause) **win** the hard way. Get ready. Signal for each sound
   as the children say *www* (pause) *iii* (pause) *nnn*. The children are
   to pause two seconds between the sounds. Repeat until firm.
b. Everybody, write the word (pause) **win**. Check children's
   responses.

TASK 3   Children write **and**

You're going to write the word **and**. Think about the sounds in
(pause) **and** and write the word. Check children's responses.

TASK 4   Children write **ant**

a. You're going to write the word (pause) **ant**. Say the sounds you
   write for (pause) **ant**. Get ready. Signal for each sound as the
   children say *aaa* (pause) *nnn* (pause) *t*. The children are to pause
   two seconds between the sounds. Repeat until firm.
b. Everybody, write the word (pause) **ant**. Check children's
   responses.

TASK 5   Children write **we, sit, he, fat**

a. You're going to write the word **we**. Think about the sounds in
   (pause) **we** and write the word. Check children's responses.
b. Repeat *a* for **sit, he,** and **fat.**

END OF SPELLING LESSON

Spelling Lesson 47

WORD WRITING

TASK 1   Children write **me, has**

a. You're going to write the word **me**. Think about the sounds in
   (pause) **me** and write the word. Check children's responses.

To correct	1. Say the sounds in **me**. (Signal.) *Mmmēēē.*
	2. Say the sounds the hard way. (Signal.) *Mmm*
	(pause) *ēēē.*
	3. Write the word **me**. Check children's responses.

b. Now you're going to write the word **has**. Think about the sounds
   in (pause) **has** and write the word. Check children's responses.

To correct	1. Say the sounds the hard way. (Signal.) *H* (pause)
	aaa (pause) *sss.*
	2. Write the word **has**. Check children's responses.

TASK 2   Children write **was**

a. You're going to write the word (pause) **was**. When you write the
   word (pause) **was,** you write these sounds. **Www** (pause) **aaa**
   (pause) **sss.**
b. Say the sounds you write for (pause) **was**. Signal for each sound
   as the children say *www* (pause) *aaa* (pause) *sss*. The children are
   to pause two seconds between the sounds. Repeat until firm.
c. Everybody, write the word (pause) **was**. Check children's
   responses.

TASK 3   Children write we

You're going to write the word **we**. Think about the sounds in (pause) **we** and write the word.   Check children's responses.

TASK 4   Children write dad

a. You're going to write the word **dad**. Listen. **Dad**. Saying the sounds in (pause) **dad** the hard way. Get ready.   Signal for each sound as the children say *d* (pause) *aaa* (pause) *d.* The children are to pause two seconds between the sounds. Repeat until firm.

b. Everybody, write the word (pause) **dad**. Check children's responses.

TASK 5   Children write tin, an, ant

a. You're going to write the word **tin**. Think about the sounds in (pause) **tin** and write the word.   Check children's responses.

To correct	1. Say the sounds in **tin**. (Signal.) *Tiiinnn.*
	2. Say the sounds the hard way. (Signal.) *T* (pause) *iii* (pause) *nnn.*
	3. Write the word **tin**. Check children's responses.

b. Repeat *a* for **an** and **ant**.

END OF SPELLING LESSON

Spelling Lesson 48

WORD WRITING

TASK 1   Children write we

a. You're going to write the word **we**. Think about the sounds in (pause) **we** and write the word.   Check children's responses.

To correct	1. Say the sounds in **we**. (Signal.) *Wwwēēē.*
	2. Say the sounds the hard way. (Signal.) *Www* (pause) *ēēē.*
	3. Write the word **we**. Check children's responses.

b. Now you're going to write the word **has**. Think about the sounds in (pause) **has** and write the word.   Check children's responses.

To correct	1. Say the sounds the hard way. (Signal.) *H* (pause) *aaa* (pause) *sss.*
	2. Write the word **has**. Check children's responses.

TASK 2   Children write was

a. You're going to write the word (pause) **was**. When you write the word (pause) **was**, you write these sounds. **Www** (pause) **aaa** (pause) **sss**.

b. Say the sounds you write for (pause) **was**. Signal for each sound as the children say *www* (pause) *aaa* (pause) *sss.* The children are to pause two seconds between sounds. Repeat until firm.

c. Everybody, write the word (pause) **was**. Check children's responses.

TASK 3   Children write tin, land, sand

a. You're going to write the word **tin**. Think about the sounds in (pause) **tin** and write the word.   Check children's responses.

b. Repeat *a* for **land** and **sand**.

END OF SPELLING LESSON

Spelling Lesson 49

WORD WRITING

TASK 1   Children write has

You're going to write the word **has**. Think about the sounds in (pause) **has** and write the word.   Check children's responses.

To correct	1. Say the sounds the hard way. (Signal.) *H* (pause) *aaa* (pause) *sss.*
	2. Write the word **has**. Check children's responses.

TASK 2   Children write was

a. You're going to write the word (pause) **was**. When you write the word (pause) **was**, you write these sounds. **Www** (pause) **aaa** (pause) **sss**.

b. Say the sounds you write for (pause) **was**. Signal for each sound as the children say *www* (pause) *aaa* (pause) *sss*. The children are to pause two seconds between sounds. Repeat until firm.

c. Everybody, write the word (pause) **was**. Check children's responses.

TASK 3   Children write hid, did, dad, tin

a. You're going to write the word **hid**. Think about the sounds in (pause) **hid** and write the word. Check children's responses.

To correct	1. Say the sounds in **hid**. *Hiiid.*
	2. Say the sounds the hard way. *H* (pause) *iii* (pause) *d.*
	3. Write the word **hid**. Check children's responses.

b. Repeat *a* for **did, dad,** and **tin**.

END OF SPELLING LESSON

Spelling Lesson 50

WORD WRITING

TASK 1   Children write is, has, his

a. You're going to write the word **is**. Think about the sounds in (pause) **is** and write the word. Check children's responses.

| To correct | 1. Say the sounds the hard way. (Signal.) *Iii* (pause) *sss.* |
| | 2. Write the word **is**. Check children's responses. |

b. Repeat *a* for **has** and **his**.

TASK 2   Children write was

a. You're going to write the word (pause) **was**. Say the sounds you write for (pause) **was**. Get ready. Signal for each sound as the children say *www* (pause) *aaa* (pause) *sss*. The children are to pause two seconds between the sounds. Repeat until firm.

b. Everybody, write the word (pause) **was**. Check children's responses.

SENTENCE WRITING

TASK 3   Children write a sentence

a. Listen to this sentence. **He hit me.** Your turn. Say that sentence. Get ready. (Signal.) *He hit me.*

b. Now you're going to say it the slow way. Get ready. Signal for each word as the children say *he* (pause) *hit* (pause) *me*. Repeat until firm.

c. Everybody, write the sentence. Spell each word the right way. As you check children's responses, remind the children: Don't forget to put a period at the end of your sentence.

END OF SPELLING LESSON

Spelling Lesson 51

SOUND WRITING

TASK 1   Children write c

a. You're going to write a sound.

b. Here's the sound you're going to write. Listen. *c.* What sound? (Signal.) *c.*

c. Write **c** on the board. Here's the **c** you're going to write. Then erase **c**.

d. Write **c**. Check children's responses.

WORD WRITING

TASK 2   Children write was

a. You're going to write the word (pause) **was**. Say the sounds you write for (pause) **was**. Get ready. Signal for each sound as the children say *www* (pause) *aaa* (pause) *sss*. The children are to pause two seconds between the sounds. Repeat until firm.
b. Everybody, write the word (pause) **was**. Check children's responses.

TASK 3   Children write tin, did, we

a. You're going to write the word **tin**. Think about the sounds in (pause) **tin** and write the word. Check children's responses.

To correct	1. Say the sounds in **tin**. (Signal.) *Tiiinnn.*
	2. Say the sounds the hard way. (Signal.) *T* (pause) *iii* (pause) *nnn.*
	3. Write the word **tin**. Check children's responses.

b. Repeat *a* for **did** and **we**.

SENTENCE WRITING

TASK 4   Children write a sentence

a. Listen to this sentence. **We had sand.** Your turn. Say that sentence. Get ready. (Signal.) *We had sand.*
b. Now you're going to say it the slow way. Get ready. Signal for each word as the children say *we* (pause) *had* (pause) *sand.* Repeat until firm.
c. Everybody, write the sentence. Spell each word the right way. As you check children's responses, remind the children: **Don't forget to put a period at the end of your sentence.**

END OF SPELLING LESSON

Spelling Lesson 52

SOUND WRITING

TASK 1   Children write c

a. You're going to write a sound.
b. Here's the sound you're going to write. Listen. **c.**
What sound? (Signal.) *c.*
c. Write **c** on the board. Here's the **c** you're going to write. Then erase **c.**
d. Write **c.** Check children's responses.

WORD WRITING

TASK 2   Children write can

a. You're going to write the word (pause) **can**. This word is tough. I'll say the sounds in (pause) **can** the hard way. Listen. **C** (pause) **aaa** (pause) **nnn.**
b. Your turn. Say the sounds in (pause) **can**. Get ready. Signal for each sound as the children say *c* (pause) *aaa* (pause) *nnn*. The children are to pause two seconds between sounds. Repeat until firm.
c. Everybody, write the word (pause) **can**. Check children's responses.

TASK 3   Children write has

You're going to write the word **has**. Think about the sounds in (pause) **has** and write the word. Check children's responses.

To correct	1. Say the sounds the hard way. (Signal.) *H* (pause) *aaa* (pause) *sss.*
	2. Write the word **has**. Check children's responses.

TASK 4   Children write was

a. You're going to write the word (pause) **was**. Say the sounds you write for (pause) **was**. Get ready. Signal for each sound as the children say *www* (pause) *aaa* (pause) *sss*. The children are to pause two seconds between the sounds. Repeat until firm.
b. Everybody, write the word (pause) **was**. Check responses.

TASK 5 Children write land, nut

a. You're going to write the word **land**. Think about the sounds in
(pause) **land** and write the word. Check children's responses.

To correct	1. Say the sounds in **land**. (Signal.) *Lllaaannnd*.
	2. Say the sounds the hard way. (Signal.) *Lll* (pause) *aaa* (pause) *nnn* (pause) *d*.
	3. Write the word **land**. Check children's responses.

b. Repeat *a* for **nut**.

SENTENCE WRITING

TASK 6 Children write a sentence

a. Listen to this sentence. **He had fun**. Your turn. Say that
sentence. Get ready. (Signal.) *He had fun*.

b. Now you're going to say it the slow way. Get ready. Signal for
each word as the children say *he* (pause) *had* (pause) *fun*.
Repeat until firm.

c. Everybody, write the sentence. Spell each word the right way. As
you check children's responses, remind the children: Don't forget
to put a period at the end of your sentence.

END OF SPELLING LESSON

Spelling Lesson 53

WORD WRITING

TASK 1 Children write can

a. You're going to write the word (pause) **can**. This word is tough.
I'll say the sounds in (pause) **can** the hard way. Listen.
C (pause) **aaa** (pause) **nnn**.

b. Your turn. Say the sounds in (pause) **can**. Get ready.
Signal for each sound as the children say *c* (pause) *aaa* (pause)
nnn. The children are to pause two seconds between the sounds.
Repeat until firm.

c. Everybody, write the word (pause) **can**. Check responses.

TASK 2 Children write arm

a. You're going to write the word (pause) **arm**. When you write the
word (pause) **arm**, you write these sounds. **Aaa** (pause) **rrr**
(pause) **mmm**.

b. Say the sounds you write for (pause) **arm**. Signal for each
sound as the children say *aaa* (pause) *rrr* (pause) *mmm*. The
children are to pause two seconds between the sounds.
Repeat until firm.

c. Everybody, write the word (pause) **arm**. Check children's
responses.

TASK 3 Children write sand, fit, mud, tin

a. You're going to write the word **sand**. Think about the sounds in
(pause) **sand** and write the word. Check children's responses.

To correct	1. Say the sounds in **sand**. (Signal.) *Sssaaannnd*.
	2. Say the sounds the hard way. (Signal.) *Sss* (pause) *aaa* (pause) *nnn* (pause) *d*.
	3. Write the word **sand**. Check children's responses.

b. Repeat *a* for **fit, mud,** and **tin**.

SENTENCE WRITING

TASK 4 Children write a sentence

a. Listen to this sentence. **He was mad**. Your turn. Say that sentence.
Get ready. (Signal.) *He was mad*.

b. Now you're going to say it the slow way. Get ready. Signal for
each word as the children say *he* (pause) *was* (pause) *mad*.
Repeat until firm.

c. Everybody, write the sentence. Spell each word the right way.
As you check children's responses, remind the children: Don't
forget to put a period at the end of your sentence.

END OF SPELLING LESSON

Spelling Lesson 54

WORD WRITING

TASK 1   Children write **if, am**

a. You're going to write the word **if**. Think about the sounds in (pause) **if** and write the word. Check children's responses.

To correct	1. Say the sounds in **if**. (Signal.) *Iiifff*.
	2. Say the sounds the hard way. (Signal.) *Iii* (pause) *fff*.
	3. Write the word **if**. Check children's responses.

b. Repeat *a* for **am**.

TASK 2   Children write **arm, farm**

a. You're going to write the word (pause) **arm**. When you write the word (pause) **arm**, you write these sounds. **Aaa** (pause) **rrr** (pause) **mmm**.

b. Say the sounds you write for (pause) **arm**. Signal for each sound as the children say *aaa* (pause) *rrr* (pause) *mmm*. The children are to pause two seconds between sounds. Repeat until firm.

c. Everybody, write the word (pause) **arm**. Check children's responses.

d. Now you're going to write the word (pause) **farm**. When you write the word (pause) **farm**, you write these sounds. **Fff** (pause) **aaa** (pause) **rrr** (pause) **mmm**.

e. Say the sounds you write for (pause) **farm**. Signal for each sound as the children say *fff* (pause) *aaa* (pause) *rrr* (pause) *mmm*. The children are to pause two seconds between sounds. Repeat until firm.

f. Everybody, write the word (pause) **farm**. Check children's responses.

TASK 3   Children write **can**

a. You're going to write the word (pause) **can**. This word is tough. I'll say the sounds in (pause) **can** the hard way. Listen. **C** (pause) **aaa** (pause) **nnn**.

b. Your turn. Say the sounds in (pause) **can**. Get ready. Signal for each sound as the children say *c* (pause) *aaa* (pause) *nnn*. The children are to pause two seconds between the sounds. Repeat until firm.

c. Everybody, write the word (pause) **can**. Check children's responses.

TASK 4   Children write **did**

You're going to write the word **did**. Think about the sounds in (pause) **did** and write the word. Check children's responses.

To correct	1. Say the sounds in **did**. (Signal.) *Diiid*.
	2. Say the sounds the hard way. (Signal.) *D* (pause) *iii* (pause) *d*.
	3. Write the word **did**. Check children's responses.

SENTENCE WRITING

TASK 5   Children write a sentence

a. Listen to this sentence. **He was fat**. Say the sentence. Get ready. (Signal.) *He was fat.*

b. Now you're going to say it the slow way. Get ready. Signal for each word as the children say *he* (pause) *was* (pause) *fat*. Repeat until firm.

c. Everybody, write the sentence. Spell each word the right way. As you check children's responses, remind the children: Don't forget to put a period at the end of your sentence.

END OF SPELLING LESSON

Spelling Lesson 55

WORD WRITING

TASK 1   Children write **ant, sun, can**

a. You're going to write the word **ant**. Think about the sounds in (pause) **ant** and write the word.   Check children's responses.

To correct	1. Say the sounds in **ant**. (Signal.) *Aaannnt.*
	2. Say the sounds the hard way. (Signal.) *Aaa* (pause) *nnn* (pause) *t.*
	3. Write the word **ant**. Check children's responses.

b. Repeat *a* for **sun** and **can**.

TASK 2   Children write **arm, farm**

a. You're going to write the word (pause) **arm**. When you write the word (pause) **arm**, you write these sounds. **Aaa** (pause) **rrr** (pause) **mmm**.

b. Say the sounds you write for (pause) **arm**. Signal for each sound as the children say *aaa* (pause) *rrr* (pause) *mmm*. The children are to pause two seconds between sounds. Repeat until firm.

c. Everybody, write the word (pause) **arm**. Check children's responses.

d. Now you're going to write the word (pause) **farm**. When you write the word (pause) **farm**, you write these sounds. **Fff** (pause) **aaa** (pause) **rrr** (pause) **mmm**.

e. Say the sounds you write for (pause) **farm**. Signal for each sound as the children say *fff* (pause) *aaa* (pause) *rrr* (pause) *mmm*. The children are to pause two seconds between sounds. Repeat until firm.

f. Everybody, write the word (pause) **farm**. Check children's responses.

TASK 3   Children write **hot**

You're going to write the word **hot**. Think about the sounds in (pause) **hot** and write the word.   Check children's responses.

SENTENCE WRITING

TASK 4   Children write a sentence

a. Listen to this sentence. **It is a nut**. Your turn. Say the sentence. Get ready.   (Signal.) *It is a nut.*

b. Now you're going to say it the slow way. Get ready.   Signal for each word as the children say *it* (pause) *is* (pause) *a* (pause) *nut*. Repeat until firm.

c. Everybody, write the sentence. Spell each word the right way. As you check children's responses, remind the children: Don't forget to put a period at the end of your sentence.

END OF SPELLING LESSON

Spelling Lesson 56

WORD WRITING

TASK 1   Children write **arm**

a. You're going to write the word (pause) **arm**. Say the sounds you write for (pause) **arm**. Get ready.   Signal for each sound as the children say *aaa* (pause) *rrr* (pause) *mmm*. The children are to pause two seconds between the sounds. Repeat until firm.

b. Everybody, write the word (pause) **arm**. Check children's responses.

TASK 2   Children write **not, and**

a. You're going to write the word **not**. Think about the sounds in (pause) **not** and write the word.   Check children's responses.

To correct	1. Say the sounds in **not**. (Signal.) *Nnnooot.*
	2. Say the sounds the hard way. (Signal.) *Nnn* (pause) *ooo* (pause) *t.*
	3. Write the word **not**. Check children's responses.

b. Repeat *a* for **and**.

TASK 3   Children write **farm**

a. You're going to write the word (pause) **farm**. Say the sounds you write for (pause) **farm**. Get ready. Signal for each sound as the children say *fff* (pause) *aaa* (pause) *rrr* (pause) *mmm*. The children are to pause two seconds between the sounds. Repeat until firm.

b. Everybody, write the word (pause) **farm**. Check children's responses.

TASK 4   Children write **hid**

You're going to write the word **hid**. Think about the sounds in (pause) **hid** and write the word. Check children's responses.

SENTENCE WRITING

TASK 5   Children write a sentence

a. Listen to this sentence. **It is hot**. Your turn. Say the sentence. Get ready. (Signal.) *It is hot.*

b. Now you're going to say it the slow way. Get ready. Signal for each word as the children say *it* (pause) *is* (pause) *hot.* Repeat until firm.

c. Everybody, write the sentence. Spell each word the right way. Check children's responses.

END OF SPELLING LESSON

Spelling Lesson 57

WORD WRITING

TASK 1   Children write **farm**

a. You're going to write the word (pause) **farm**. Say the sounds you write for (pause) **farm**. Get ready. Signal for each sound as the children say *fff* (pause) *aaa* (pause) *rrr* (pause) *mmm*. The children are to pause two seconds between the sounds. Repeat until firm.

b. Everybody, write the word (pause) **farm**. Check responses

TASK 2   Children write **can**

You're going to write the word **can**. Think about the sounds in (pause) **can** and write the word. Check children's responses.

To correct	1. Say the sounds in **can**. (Signal.) *Caaannn.*
	2. Say the sounds the hard way. (Signal.) *C* (pause) *aaa* (pause) *nnn.*
	3. Write the word **can**. Check children's responses.

TASK 3   Children write **car**

a. You're going to write the word (pause) **car**. When you write the word (pause) **car**, you write these sounds. **C** (pause) **aaa** (pause) **rrr**.

b. Say the sounds you write for (pause) **car**. Signal for each sound as the children say *c* (pause) *aaa* (pause) *rrr.* The children are to pause two seconds between sounds. Repeat until firm.

c. Everybody, write the word (pause) **car**. Check children's responses.

TASK 4   Children write **me, sand, hid**

a. You're going to write the word **me**. Think about the sounds in (pause) **me** and write the word. Check children's responses.

b. Repeat *a* for **sand** and **hid**.

SENTENCE WRITING

TASK 5   Children write a sentence

a. Listen to this sentence. **He had a fan**. Your turn. Say the sentence. Get ready. (Signal.) *He had a fan.*

b. Now you're going to say it the slow way. Get ready. Signal for each word as the children say *he* (pause) *had* (pause) *a* (pause) *fan.* Repeat until firm.

c. Everybody, write the sentence. Spell each word the right way. Check children's responses.

END OF SPELLING LESSON

Spelling Lesson 58

WORD WRITING

TASK 1   Children write **and, mud, hot**

a. You're going to write the word **and**. Think about the sounds in (pause) **and** and write the word. Check children's responses.

To correct	1. Say the sounds in **and**. (Signal.) *Aaannnd*.
	2. Say the sounds the hard way. (Signal.) *Aaa* (pause) *nnn* (pause) *d*.
	3. Write the word **and**. Check children's responses.

b. Repeat *a* for **mud** and **hot**.

TASK 2   Children write **arm**

a. You're going to write the word (pause) **arm**. Say the sounds you write for (pause) **arm**. Get ready. Signal for each sound as the children say *aaa* (pause) *rrr* (pause) *mmm*. The children are to pause two seconds between the sounds. Repeat until firm.

b. Everybody, write the word (pause) **arm**. Check children's responses.

TASK 3   Children write **car**

a. You're going to write the word (pause) **car**. When you write the word (pause) **car**, you write these sounds. C (pause) **aaa** (pause) **rrr**.

b. Say the sounds you write for (pause) **car**. Signal for each sound as the children say *c* (pause) *aaa* (pause) *rrr*. The children are to pause two seconds between sounds. Repeat until firm.

c. Everybody, write the word (pause) **car**. Check children's responses.

TASK 4   Children write **can**

You're going to write the word **can**. Think about the sounds in (pause) **can** and write the word. Check children's responses.

SENTENCE WRITING

TASK 5   Children write a sentence

a. Listen to this sentence. **His dad is sad**. Your turn. Say the sentence. Get ready. (Signal.) *His dad is sad.*

b. Now you're going to say it the slow way. Get ready. Signal for each word as the children say *his* (pause) *dad* (pause) *is* (pause) *sad.* Repeat until firm.

c. Everybody, write the sentence. Spell each word the right way. Check children's responses.

END OF SPELLING LESSON

Spelling Lesson 59

WORD WRITING

TASK 1   Children write **car, far, tar**

a. You're going to write the word (pause) **car**. When you write the word (pause) **car**, you write these sounds. C (pause) **aaa** (pause) **rrr**.

b. Say the sounds you write for (pause) **car**. Signal for each sound as the children say *c* (pause) *aaa* (pause) *rrr*. The children are to pause two seconds between sounds. Repeat until firm.

c. Everybody, write the word (pause) **car**. Check responses.

d. Now you're going to write the word (pause) **far**. When you write the word (pause) **far**, you write these sounds. Fff (pause) **aaa** (pause) **rrr**.

e. Say the sounds you write for (pause) **far**. Signal for each sound as the children say *fff* (pause) *aaa* (pause) *rrr*. The children are to pause two seconds between sounds. Repeat until firm.

f. Everybody, write the word (pause) **far**. Check responses.

g. Next you're going to write the word (pause) **tar**. When you write the word (pause) **tar**, you write these sounds. T (pause) **aaa** (pause) **rrr**.

h. Say the sounds you write for (pause) **tar**. Signal for each sound as the children say *t* (pause) *aaa* (pause) *rrr*. The children are to pause two seconds between sounds. Repeat until firm.

i. Everybody, write the word (pause) **tar**. Check responses.

TASK 2   Children write **arm, farm**

a. You're going to write the word **arm**. Think about the sounds in (pause) **arm** and write the word. Check children's responses.

| To correct | 1. Say the sounds the hard way. (Signal.) *Aaa* (pause) *rrr* (pause) *mmm*. |
| | 2. Write the word **arm**. Check children's responses. |

b. Repeat *a* for **farm**.

SENTENCE WRITING

TASK 3   Children write a sentence

a. Listen to this sentence. **His dad has sand**. Your turn. Say that sentence. Get ready. (Signal.) *His dad has sand*.

b. Now you're going to say it the slow way. Get ready. Signal for each word as the children say *his* (pause) *dad* (pause) *has* (pause) *sand*. Repeat until firm.

c. Everybody, write the sentence. Spell each word the right way. Check children's responses.

END OF SPELLING LESSON

Spelling Lesson 60

WORD WRITING

TASK 1   Children write **are**

a. You're going to write the word (pause) **are**. When you write the word (pause) **are**, you write these sounds. **Aaa** (pause) **rrr** (pause) **ēēē**.

b. Say the sounds you write for (pause) **are**. Signal for each sound as the children say *aaa* (pause) *rrr* (pause) *ēēē*. The children are to pause two seconds between sounds. Repeat until firm.

c. Everybody, write the word (pause) **are**. Check children's responses.

TASK 2   Children write **far, car**

a. You're going to write the word (pause) **far**. Say the sounds you write for (pause) **far**. Get ready. Signal for each sound as the children say *fff* (pause) *aaa* (pause) *rrr*. The children are to pause two seconds between the sounds. Repeat until firm.

b. Everybody, write the word (pause) **far**. Check children's responses.

c. Now you're going to write the word (pause) **car**. Say the sounds you write for (pause) **car**. Signal for each sound as the children say *c* (pause) *aaa* (pause) *rrr*. The children are to pause two seconds between sounds. Repeat until firm.

d. Everybody, write the word (pause) **car**. Check children's responses.

TASK 3   Children write **not, land**

a. You're going to write the word **not**. Think about the sounds in (pause) **not** and write the word. Check children's responses.

To correct	1. Say the sounds in **not**. (Signal.) *Nnnooot*.
	2. Say the sounds the hard way. (Signal.) *Nnn* (pause) *ooo* (pause) *t*.
	3. Write the word **not**. Check children's responses.

b. Repeat *a* for **land**.

SENTENCE WRITING

TASK 4   Children write a sentence

a. Listen to this sentence. **He has a dad**. Your turn. Say that sentence. Get ready. (Signal.) *He has a dad*.

b. Now you're going to say it the slow way. Get ready. Signal for each word as the children say *he* (pause) *has* (pause) *a* (pause) *dad*. Repeat until firm.

c. Everybody, write the sentence. Spell each word the right way. Check children's responses.

END OF SPELLING LESSON

Spelling Lesson 61

WORD WRITING

TASK 1   Children write **car**

a. You're going to write the word (pause) **car**. Say the sounds you write for (pause) **car**. Get ready. Signal for each sound as the children say *c* (pause) *aaa* (pause) *rrr*. The children are to pause two seconds between the sounds. Repeat until firm.

b. Everybody, write the word (pause) **car**. Check children's responses.

TASK 2   Children write **tan**

You're going to write the word **tan**. Think about the sounds in (pause) **tan** and write the word. Check children's responses.

To correct	1. Say the sounds in **tan**. (Signal.) *Taaannn.*
	2. Say the sounds the hard way. (Signal.) *T* (pause) *aaa* (pause) *nnn.*
	3. Write the word **tan**. Check children's responses.

TASK 3   Children write **are**

a. You're going to write the word (pause) **are**. When you write the word (pause) **are**, you write these sounds. **Aaa** (pause) **rrr** (pause) **ēēē**.

b. Say the sounds you write for (pause) **are**. Signal for each sound as the children say *aaa* (pause) *rrr* (pause) *ēēē*. The children are to pause two seconds between sounds. Repeat until firm.

c. Write the word (pause) **are**. Check children's responses.

TASK 4   Children write **was, can**

a. You're going to write the word **was**. Think about the sounds in (pause) **was** and write the word. Check children's responses.

| To correct | 1. Say the sounds the hard way. (Signal.) *Www* (pause) *aaa* (pause) *sss.* |
| | 2. Write the word **was**. Check children's responses. |

b. Repeat *a* for **can.**

TASK 5   Children write **far**

a. You're going to write the word (pause) **far**. Say the sounds you write for (pause) **far**. Get ready. Signal for each sound as the children say *fff* (pause) *aaa* (pause) *rrr.* The children are to pause two seconds between the sounds. Repeat until firm.

b. Everybody, write the word (pause) **far**. Check children's responses.

SENTENCE WRITING

TASK 6   Children write a sentence

a. Listen to this sentence. **A farm is fun.** Your turn. Say that sentence. Get ready. (Signal.) *A farm is fun.*

b. Now you're going to say it the slow way. Get ready. Signal for each word as the children say *a* (pause) *farm* (pause) *is* (pause) *fun.* Repeat until firm.

c. Everybody, write the sentence. Spell each word the right way. Check children's responses.

END OF SPELLING LESSON

Spelling Lesson 62

WORD WRITING

TASK 1   Children write **are**

a. You're going to write the word (pause) **are**. Say the sounds you write for (pause) **are**. Get ready. Signal for each sound as the children say *aaa* (pause) *rrr* (pause) *ēēē*. The children are to pause two seconds between the sounds. Repeat until firm.

b. Everybody, write the word (pause) **are**. Check children's responses.

TASK 2   Children write **hard**

a. You're going to write the word (pause) **hard**. When you write the word (pause) **hard**, you write these sounds. **H** (pause) **aaa** (pause) **rrr** (pause) **d**.

b. Say the sounds you write for (pause) **hard**. Signal for each sound as the children say *h* (pause) *aaa* (pause) *rrr* (pause) *d.* The children are to pause two seconds between sounds. Repeat until firm.

c. Everybody, write the word (pause) **hard**. Check children's responses.

TASK 3   Children write **car**

a. You're going to write the word (pause) **car**. Say the sounds you write for (pause) **car**. Get ready. Signal for each sound as the children say *c* (pause) *aaa* (pause) *rrr.* The children are to pause two seconds between the sounds. Repeat until firm.

b. Everybody, write the word (pause) **car**. Check children's responses.

TASK 4   Children write **card**

a. You're going to write the word (pause) **card**. When you write the word (pause) **card**, you write these sounds. **C** (pause) **aaa** (pause) **rrr** (pause) **d**.

b. Say the sounds you write for (pause) **card**. Signal for each sound as the children say *c* (pause) *aaa* (pause) *rrr* (pause) *d.* The children are to pause two seconds between the sounds. Repeat until firm.

c. Everybody, write the word (pause) **card**. Check children's responses.

TASK 5   Children write **nod**

You're going to write the word **nod**. Think about the sounds in (pause) **nod** and write the word. Check children's responses.

To correct	**1.** Say the sounds in **nod**. (Signal.) *Nnnooood.* **2.** Say the sounds the hard way. (Signal.) *Nnn* (pause) *ooo* (pause) *d.* **3.** Write the word **nod**. Check children's responses.

SENTENCE WRITING

TASK 6   Children write a sentence

a. Listen to this sentence. **I am not sad**. Your turn. Say that sentence. Get ready. (Signal.) *I am not sad.*

b. Now you're going to say it the slow way. Get ready. Signal for each word as the children say *I* (pause) *am* (pause) *not* (pause) *sad.* Repeat until firm.

c. Everybody, write the sentence. Spell each word the right way. Check children's responses.

END OF SPELLING LESSON

Spelling Lesson 63

SOUND WRITING

TASK 1   Children write **b**

a. You're going to write a sound.

b. Here's the sound you're going to write. Listen. **b**. What sound? (Signal.) *b.*

c. Write **b**. Check children's responses.

WORD WRITING

TASK 2   Children write **we**, **hid**

a. You're going to write the word **we**. Think about the sounds in (pause) **we** and write the word. Check children's responses.

To correct	**1.** Say the sounds in **we**. (Signal.) *Wwwēēē.* **2.** Say the sounds the hard way. (Signal.) *Www* (pause) *ēēē.* **3.** Write the word **we**. Check children's responses.

b. Repeat *a* for **hid**.

TASK 3   Children write **are**

a. You're going to write the word (pause) **are.** Say the sounds you write for (pause) **are.** Get ready. Signal for each sound as the children say *aaa* (pause) *rrr* (pause) *ēēē.* The children are to pause two seconds between the sounds. Repeat until firm.

b. Everybody, write the word (pause) **are.** Check children's responses.

TASK 4   Children write **was, has, can**

a. You're going to write the word **was.** Think about the sounds in (pause) **was** and write the word. Check children's responses.

To correct	1. Say the sounds the hard way. (Signal.) *Www* (pause) *aaa* (pause) *sss.*
	2. Write the word **was.** Check children's responses.

b. Repeat *a* for **has** and **can.**

SENTENCE WRITING

TASK 5   Children write a sentence

a. Listen to this sentence. **His dad was mad.** Your turn. Say that sentence. Get ready. (Signal.) *His dad was mad.*

b. Now you're going to say it the slow way. Get ready. Signal for each word as the children say *his* (pause) *dad* (pause) *was* (pause) *mad.* Repeat until firm.

c. Everybody, write the sentence. Spell each word the right way. Check children's responses.

END OF SPELLING LESSON

Spelling Lesson 64

SOUND WRITING

TASK 1   Children write **b**

a. You're going to write a sound.

b. Here's the sound you're going to write. Listen. **b.** What sound? (Signal.) *b.*

c. Write **b.** Check children's responses.

WORD WRITING

TASK 2   Children write **are, sit**

a. You're going to write the word **are.** Think about the sounds in (pause) **are** and write the word. Check children's responses.

To correct	1. Say the sounds the hard way. (Signal.) *Aaa* (pause) *rrr* (pause) *ēēē.*
	2. Write the word **are.** Check children's responses.

b. Repeat *a* for **sit.**

TASK 3   Children write **bit**

a. You're going to write the word (pause) **bit.** This word is tough. I'll say the sounds in (pause) **bit** the hard way. Listen. **B** (pause) **iii** (pause) **t.**

b. Your turn. Say the sounds in (pause) **bit.** Get ready. Signal for each sound as the children say *b* (pause) *iii* (pause) *t.* The children are to pause two seconds between sounds. Repeat until firm.

c. Everybody, write the word (pause) **bit.** Check children's responses.

TASK 4   Children write **land**

You're going to write the word **land.** Think about the sounds in (pause) **land** and write the word. Check children's responses.

41

TASK 5   Children write card

a. You're going to write the word (pause) **card**. Say the sounds you write for (pause) **card**. Get ready. Signal for each sound as the children say *c* (pause) *aaa* (pause) *rrr* (pause) *d*. The children are to pause two seconds between the sounds. Repeat until firm.

b. Everybody, write the word (pause) **card**. Check children's responses.

TASK 6   Children write cat

a. You're going to write the word **cat**. Listen. **Cat**. Saying the sounds in (pause) **cat** the hard way. Get ready. Signal for each sound as the children say *c* (pause) *aaa* (pause) *t*. The children are to pause two seconds between the sounds. Repeat until firm.

b. Everybody, write the word (pause) **cat**. Check children's responses.

SENTENCE WRITING

TASK 7   Children write a sentence

a. Listen to this sentence. **I am not fat**. Your turn. Say that sentence. Get ready. (Signal.) *I am not fat*.

b. Now you're going to say it the slow way. Get ready. Signal for each word as the children say *I* (pause) *am* (pause) *not* (pause) *fat*. Repeat until firm.

c. Everybody, write the sentence. Spell each word the right way. Check children's responses.

END OF SPELLING LESSON

Spelling Lesson 65

WORD WRITING

TASK 1   Children write card, farm, is

a. You're going to write the word **card**. Think about the sounds in (pause) **card** and write the word. Check children's responses.

To correct	1. Say the sounds the hard way. (Signal.) *C* (pause) *aaa* (pause) *rrr* (pause) *d*.
	2. Write the word **card**. Check children's responses.

b. Repeat a for **farm** and **is**.

TASK 2   Children write bit

a. You're going to write the word (pause) **bit**. This word is tough. I'll say the sounds in (pause) **bit** the hard way. Listen. **B** (pause) *iii* (pause) *t*.

b. Your turn. Say the sounds in (pause) **bit**. Get ready. Signal for each sound as the children say *b* (pause) *iii* (pause) *t*. The children are to pause two seconds between the sounds. Repeat until firm.

c. Everybody, write the word (pause) **bit**. Check children's responses.

TASK 3   Children write not

You're going to write the word **not**. Think about the sounds in (pause) **not** and write the word.

To correct	1. Say the sounds in **not**. (Signal.) *Nnnooot*.
	2. Say the sounds the hard way. (Signal.) *Nnn* (pause) *ooo* (pause) *t*.
	3. Write the word **not**. Check children's responses.

SENTENCE WRITING

TASK 4 Children write a sentence

a. Listen to this sentence. **He did run far**. Your turn. Say that sentence. Get ready. (Signal.) *He did run far*.

b. Now you're going to say it the slow way. Get ready. Signal for each word as the children say *he* (pause) *did* (pause) *run* (pause) *far*. Repeat until firm.

c. Everybody, write the sentence. Spell each word the right way. Check children's responses.

END OF SPELLING LESSON

Spelling Lesson 66

WORD WRITING

TASK 1 Children write **bad**

a. You're going to write the word (pause) **bad**. This word is tough. I'll say the sounds in (pause) **bad** the hard way. Listen. **B** (pause) **aaa** (pause) **d**.

b. Your turn. Say the sounds in (pause) **bad**. Get ready. Signal for each sound as the children say *b* (pause) *aaa* (pause) *d*. The children are to pause two seconds between the sounds. Repeat until firm.

c. Everybody, write the word (pause) **bad**. Check children's responses.

TASK 2 Children write **are**, **his**, **card**

a. You're going to write the word **are**. Think about the sounds in (pause) **are** and write the word. Check children's responses.

To correct	1. Say the sounds the hard way. (Signal.) *Aaa* (pause) *rrr* (pause) *ēēē*.
	2. Write the word **are**. Check children's responses.

b. Repeat *a* for **his** and **card**.

TASK 3 Children write **cart**

a. You're going to write the word (pause) **cart**. Say the sounds you write for (pause) **cart**. Get ready. Signal for each sound as the children say *c* (pause) *aaa* (pause) *rrr* (pause) *t*. The children are to pause two seconds between the sounds. Repeat until firm.

b. Everybody, write the word (pause) **cart**. Check children's responses.

TASK 4 Children write **cat**

a. You're going to write the word **cat**. Listen. **Cat**. Saying the sounds in (pause) **cat** the hard way. Get ready. Signal for each sound as the children say *c* (pause) *aaa* (pause) *t*. The children are to pause two seconds between the sounds. Repeat until firm.

b. Everybody, write the word (pause) **cat**. Check children's responses.

SENTENCE WRITING

TASK 5 Children write a sentence

a. Listen to this sentence. **We are not sad**. Your turn. Say that sentence. Get ready. (Signal.) *We are not sad*.

b. Now you're going to say it the slow way. Get ready. Signal for each word as the children say *we* (pause) *are* (pause) *not* (pause) *sad*. Repeat until firm.

c. Everybody, write the sentence. Spell each word the right way. Check children's responses.

END OF SPELLING LESSON

Spelling Lesson 67

WORD WRITING

TASK 1   Children write **was, can**

a. You're going to write the word **was**. Think about the sounds in (pause) **was** and write the word.   Check children's responses.

To correct	1. Say the sounds the hard way. (Signal.) *Www* (pause) *aaa* (pause) *sss*.
	2. Write the word **was**. Check children's responses.

b. You're going to write the word **can**. Think about the sounds in (pause) **can** and write the word.   Check children's responses.

To correct	1. Say the sounds in **can**. (Signal.) *Caaannn*.
	2. Say the sounds the hard way. (Signal.) *C* (pause) *aaa* (pause) *nnn*.
	3. Write the word **can**. Check children's responses.

TASK 2   Children write **cat**

a. You're going to write the word **cat**. Listen. **Cat**. Saying the sounds in (pause) **cat** the hard way. Get ready.   Signal for each sound as the children say *c* (pause) *aaa* (pause) *t*. The children are to pause two seconds between the sounds. Repeat until firm.

b. Everybody, write the word (pause) **cat**. Check children's responses.

TASK 3   Children write **see**

a. You're going to write the word (pause) **see**. When you write the word (pause) **see**, you write these sounds. **Sss** (pause) *ēēē* (pause) *ēēē*.

b. Say the sounds you write for (pause) **see**. Signal for each sound as the children say *sss* (pause) *ēēē* (pause) *ēēē*. The children are to pause two seconds between sounds. Repeat until firm.

c. Write the word (pause) **see**. Check children's responses.

TASK 4   Children write **farm**

You're going to write the word **farm**. Think about the sounds in (pause) **farm** and write the word.   Check children's responses.

TASK 5   Children write **but**

a. You're going to write the word (pause) **but**. This word is tough. I'll say the sounds in (pause) **but** the hard way. Listen. **B** (pause) **uuu** (pause) *t*.

b. Your turn. Say the sounds in (pause) **but**. Get ready.   Signal for each sound as the children say *b* (pause) *uuu* (pause) *t*. The children are to pause two seconds between sounds. Repeat until firm.

c. Everybody, write the word (pause) **but**. Check children's responses.

SENTENCE WRITING

TASK 6   Children write a sentence

a. Listen to this sentence. **I am in mud**. Your turn. Say that sentence. Get ready.   (Signal.) *I am in mud.*

b. Now you're going to say it the slow way. Get ready.   Signal for each word as the children say *I* (pause) *am* (pause) *in* (pause) *mud*. Repeat until firm.

c. Everybody, write the sentence. Spell each word the right way.   Check children's responses.

END OF SPELLING LESSON

Spelling Lesson 68

WORD WRITING

TASK 1 Children write see

a. You're going to write the word (pause) **see**. When you write the word (pause) **see**, you write these sounds. **Sss** (pause) ēēē (pause) ēēē.

b. Say the sounds you write for (pause) **see**. Signal for each sound as the children say *sss* (pause) *ēēē* (pause) *ēēē*. The children are to pause two seconds between sounds. Repeat until firm.

c. Write the word (pause) **see**. Check children's responses.

TASK 2 Children write but

a. You're going to write the word (pause) **but**. This word is tough. I'll say the sounds in (pause) **but** the hard way. Listen. B (pause) **uuu** (pause) **t**.

b. Your turn. Say the sounds in (pause) **but**. Get ready. Signal for each sound as the children say *b* (pause) *uuu* (pause) *t*. The children are to pause two seconds between the sounds. Repeat until firm.

c. Everybody, write the word (pause) **but**. Check children's responses.

TASK 3 Children write his

You're going to write the word **his**. Think about the sounds in (pause) **his** and write the word. Check children's responses.

| To correct | 1. Say the sounds the hard way. (Signal.) *H* (pause) *iii* (pause) *sss*. |
| | 2. Write the word **his**. Check children's responses. |

TASK 4 Children write bit

a. You're going to write the word **bit**. Listen. **Bit**. Saying the sounds in (pause) **bit** the hard way. Get ready. Signal for each sound as the children say *b* (pause) *iii* (pause) *t*. The children are to pause two seconds between the sounds. Repeat until firm.

b. Everybody, write the word (pause) **bit**. Check children's responses.

SENTENCE WRITING

TASK 5 Children write a sentence

a. Listen to this sentence. **We are in sand**. Your turn. Say the sentence. Get ready. (Signal.) *We are in sand.*

b. Now you're going to say it the slow way. Get ready. Signal for each word as the children say *we* (pause) *are* (pause) *in* (pause) *sand*. Repeat until firm.

c. Everybody, write the sentence. Spell each word the right way. Check children's responses.

END OF SPELLING LESSON

Spelling Lesson 69

WORD WRITING

TASK 1 Children write bad

a. You're going to write the word (pause) **bad**. Say the sounds you write for (pause) **bad**. Get ready. Signal for each sound as the children say *b* (pause) *aaa* (pause) *d*. The children are to pause two seconds between the sounds. Repeat until firm.

b. Everybody, write the word (pause) **bad**. Check children's responses.

TASK 2 Children write see

a. You're going to write the word (pause) **see**. When you write the word (pause) **see**, you write these sounds. **Sss** (pause) ēēē (pause) ēēē.

b. Say the sounds you write for (pause) **see**. Signal for each sound as the children say *sss* (pause) *ēēē* (pause) *ēēē*. The children are to pause two seconds between sounds. Repeat until firm.

c. Write the word (pause) **see**. Check children's responses.

TASK 3   Children write **but**

a. You're going to write the word (pause) **but**. Say the sounds you write for (pause) **but**. Get ready. Signal for each sound as the children say *b* (pause) *uuu* (pause) *t*. The children are to pause two seconds between the sounds. Repeat until firm.

b. Everybody, write the word (pause) **but**. Check children's responses.

TASK 4   Children write **and**

You're going to write the word **and**. Think about the sounds in (pause) **and** and write the word. Check children's responses.

TASK 5   Children write **bit**

a. You're going to write the word (pause) **bit**. Say the sounds you write for (pause) **bit**. Get ready. Signal for each sound as the children say *b* (pause) *iii* (pause) *t*. The children are to pause two seconds between the sounds. Repeat until firm.

b. Everybody, write the word (pause) **bit**. Check children's responses.

SENTENCE WRITING

TASK 6   Children write a sentence

a. Listen to this sentence. **We are on land**. Your turn. Say that sentence. Get ready. (Signal.) *We are on land.*

b. Now you're going to say it the slow way. Get ready. Signal for each word as the children say *we* (pause) *are* (pause) *on* (pause) *land.* Repeat until firm.

c. Everybody, write the sentence. Spell each word the right way. Check children's responses.

END OF SPELLING LESSON

Spelling Lesson 70

SOUND WRITING

TASK 1   Children write **th**

a. You're going to write a sound.

b. Here's the sound you're going to write. Listen. **ththth**. What sound? (Signal.) *ththth.*

c. Write **ththth**. Check children's responses.

WORD WRITING

TASK 2   Children write **bit**

You're going to write the word **bit**. Think about the sounds in (pause) **bit** and write the word. Check children's responses.

To correct	1. Say the sounds in **bit**. (Signal.) *Biiit.*
	2. Say the sounds the hard way. (Signal.) *B* (pause) *iii* (pause) *t*.
	3. Write the word **bit**. Check children's responses.

TASK 3   Children write **see**

a. You're going to write the word (pause) **see**. Say the sounds you write for (pause) **see**. Get ready. Signal for each sound as the children say *sss* (pause) *ēēē* (pause) *ēēē*. The children are to pause two seconds between the sounds. Repeat until firm.

b. Everybody, write the word (pause) **see**. Check children's responses.

TASK 4   Children write **can, but, card**

a. You're going to write the word **can**. Think about the sounds in (pause) **can** and write the word. Check children's responses.

b. Repeat *a* for **but**.

c. You're going to write the word **card**. Think about the sounds in (pause) **card** and write the word.

To correct	1. Say the sounds the hard way. (Signal.) *C* (pause) *aaa* (pause) *rrr* (pause) *d*.
	2. Write the word **card**. Check children's responses.

SENTENCE WRITING

TASK 5   Children write a sentence

a. Listen to this sentence. **We had a car**. Your turn. Say that sentence. Get ready. (Signal.) *We had a car.*

b. Now you're going to say it the slow way. Get ready. Signal for each word as the children say *we* (pause) *had* (pause) *a* (pause) *car.* Repeat until firm.

c. Everybody, write the sentence. Spell each word the right way.

Check children's responses.

END OF SPELLING LESSON

Spelling Lesson 71

SOUND WRITING

TASK 1   Children write **th**

a. You're going to write a sound.

b. Here's the sound you're going to write. Listen. **ththth**.

What sound? (Signal.) *ththth.*

c. Write **ththth**. Check children's responses.

WORD WRITING

TASK 2   Children write **are, bad**

a. You're going to write the word **are**. Think about the sounds in (pause) **are** and write the word. Check children's responses.

To correct	1. Say the sounds the hard way. (Signal.) *Aaa* (pause) *rrr* (pause) *ēēē.*
	2. Write the word **are**. Check children's responses.

b. Repeat *a* for **bad**.

TASK 3   Children write **thē**

a. You're going to write the word (pause) **thē**. This word is tough. I'll say the sounds in (pause) **thē** the hard way. Listen. **Ththth** (pause) *ēēē.*

b. Your turn. Say the sounds in (pause) **thē**. Get ready. Signal for each sound as the children say *ththth* (pause) *ēēē.* The children are to pause two seconds between the sounds. Repeat until firm.

c. Everybody, write the word (pause) **thē**. Check children's responses.

TASK 4   Children write **this, that**

a. You're going to write the word **this**. Listen. **This**. Saying the sounds in (pause) **this** the hard way. Get ready. Signal for each sound as the children say *ththth* (pause) *iii* (pause) *sss.* The children are to pause two seconds between the sounds. Repeat until firm.

b. Everybody, write the word (pause) **this**. Check children's responses.

c. Repeat *a* and *b* for **that**.

SENTENCE WRITING

TASK 5   Children write a sentence

a. Listen to this sentence. **He has a farm**. Your turn. Say that sentence. Get ready. (Signal.) *He has a farm.*

b. Now you're going to say it the slow way. Get ready. Signal for each word as the children say *he* (pause) *has* (pause) *a* (pause) *farm.* Repeat until firm.

c. Everybody, write the sentence. Spell each word the right way.

Check children's responses.

END OF SPELLING LESSON

Spelling Lesson 72

WORD WRITING

TASK 1   Children write **that**

a. You're going to write the word **that**. Listen. **That**. Saying the sounds in (pause) **that** the hard way. Get ready. Signal for each sound as the children say *thththth* (pause) *aaa* (pause) *t*. The children are to pause two seconds between the sounds. Repeat until firm.

b. Everybody, write the word (pause) **that**. Check children's responses.

TASK 2   Children write **see**

a. You're going to write the word (pause) **see**. Say the sounds you write for (pause) **see**. Get ready. Signal for each sound as the children say *sss* (pause) *ēēē* (pause) *ēēē*. The children are to pause two seconds between the sounds. Repeat until firm.

b. Everybody, write the word (pause) **see**. Check children's responses.

TASK 3   Children write **the̅**

a. You're going to write the word **the̅**. Listen. **The̅**. Saying the sounds in (pause) **the̅** the hard way. Get ready. Signal for each sound as the children say *thththth* (pause) *ēēē*. The children are to pause two seconds between the sounds. Repeat until firm.

b. Everybody, write the word (pause) **the̅**. Check children's responses.

TASK 4   Children write **are**

You're going to write the word **are**. Think about the sounds in (pause) **are** and write the word. Check children's responses.

To correct	1. Say the sounds the hard way. (Signal.) *Aaa* (pause) *rrr* (pause) *ēēē*.
	2. Write the word **are**. Check children's responses.

TASK 5   Children write **this**

a. You're going to write the word **this**. Listen. **This**. Saying the sounds in (pause) **this** the hard way. Get ready. Signal for each sound as the children say *thththth* (pause) *iii* (pause) *sss*. The children are to pause two seconds between the sounds. Repeat until firm.

b. Everybody, write the word (pause) **this**. Check children's responses.

SENTENCE WRITING

TASK 6   Children write a sentence

a. Listen to this sentence. **He did not run**. Your turn. Say that sentence. Get ready. (Signal.) *He did not run*.

b. Now you're going to say it the slow way. Get ready. Signal for each word as the children say *he* (pause) *did* (pause) *not* (pause) *run*. Repeat until firm.

c. Everybody, write the sentence. Spell each word the right way. Check children's responses.

END OF SPELLING LESSON

Spelling Lesson 73

WORD WRITING

TASK 1   Children write **will**

a. You're going to write the word (pause) **will**. When you write the word (pause) **will**, you write these sounds. **Www** (pause) **iii** (pause) **lll** (pause) **lll**.

b. Say the sounds you write for (pause) **will**. Signal for each sound as the children say *www* (pause) *iii* (pause) *lll* (pause) *lll*. The children are to pause two seconds between sounds. Repeat until firm.

c. Everybody, write the word (pause) **will**. Check children's responses.

TASK 2 Children write **arm**

You're going to write the word **arm**. Think about the sounds in (pause) **arm** and write the word. Check children's responses.

| To correct | 1. Say the sounds the hard way. (Signal.) *Aaa* (pause) *rrr* (pause) *mmm*. |
| | 2. Write the word **arm**. Check children's responses. |

TASK 3 Children write **barn**

a. You're going to write the word (pause) **barn**. When you write the word (pause) **barn**, you write these sounds. **B** (pause) **aaa** (pause) **rrr** (pause) **nnn**.

b. Say the sounds you write for (pause) **barn**. Signal for each sound as the children say *b* (pause) *aaa* (pause) *rrr* (pause) *nnn*. The children are to pause two seconds between sounds. Repeat until firm.

c. Everybody, write the word (pause) **barn**. Check children's responses.

TASK 4 Children write **that**

a. You're going to write the word **that**. Listen. **That**. Saying the sounds in (pause) **that** the hard way. Get ready. Signal for each sound as the children say *ththth* (pause) *aaa* (pause) *t*. The children are to pause two seconds between the sounds. Repeat until firm.

b. Everybody, write the word (pause) **that**. Check children's responses.

TASK 5 Children write **can**

You're going to write the word **can**. Think about the sounds in (pause) **can** and write the word. Check children's responses.

SENTENCE WRITING

TASK 6 Children write a sentence

a. Listen to this sentence. **We are in the sand**. Your turn. Say that sentence. Get ready. (Signal.) *We are in the sand.*

b. Now you're going to say it the slow way. Get ready. Signal for each word as the children say *we* (pause) *are* (pause) *in* (pause) *the* (pause) *sand*. Repeat until firm.

c. Everybody, write the sentence. Spell each word the right way.

Check children's responses.

END OF SPELLING LESSON

Spelling Lesson 74

WORD WRITING

TASK 1 Children write **see**

a. You're going to write the word (pause) **see**. Say the sounds you write for (pause) **see**. Get ready. Signal for each sound as the children say *sss* (pause) *ēēē* (pause) *ēēē*. The children are to pause two seconds between the sounds. Repeat until firm.

b. Everybody, write the word (pause) **see**. Check children's responses.

TASK 2 Children write **this**

You're going to write the word **this**. Think about the sounds in (pause) **this** and write the word. Check children's responses.

To correct	1. Say the sounds in **this**. (Signal.) *Thththiiisss*.
	2. Say the sounds the hard way. (Signal.) *Ththth* (pause) *iii* (pause) *sss*.
	3. Write the word **this**. Check children's responses.

TASK 3   Children write **will**

a. You're going to write the word (pause) **will**. When you write the word (pause) **will**, you write these sounds. **Www** (pause) **iii** (pause) **lll** (pause) **lll**.

b. Say the sounds you write for (pause) **will**. Signal for each sound as the children say *www* (pause) *iii* (pause) *lll* (pause) *lll*. The children are to pause two seconds between the sounds. Repeat until firm.

c. Everybody, write the word (pause) **will**. Check responses.

TASK 4   Children write **barn**

a. You're going to write the word (pause) **barn**. Say the sounds you write for (pause) **barn**. Get ready. Signal for each sound as the children say *b* (pause) *aaa* (pause) *rrr* (pause) *nnn*. The children are to pause two seconds between the sounds. Repeat until firm.

b. Everybody, write the word (pause) **barn**. Check responses.

TASK 5   Children write **thē**, **cat**

a. You're going to write the word **thē**. Think about the sounds in (pause) **thē** and write the word. Check children's responses.

To correct	1. Say the sounds in **thē**. (Signal.) *Thththēēē*.
	2. Say the sounds the hard way. (Signal.) *Ththth* (pause) *ēēē*.
	3. Write the word **thē**. Check children's responses.

b. Repeat *a* for **cat**.

SENTENCE WRITING

TASK 6   Children write a sentence

a. Listen to this sentence. **The ant was bad**. Your turn. Say that sentence. Get ready. (Signal.) *The ant was bad.*

b. Now you're going to say it the slow way. Get ready. Signal for each word as the children say *the* (pause) *ant* (pause) *was* (pause) *bad*. Repeat until firm.

c. Everybody, write the sentence. Spell each word the right way. Check children's responses.

Spelling Lesson 75

SOUND WRITING

TASK 1   Children write **p**

a. You're going to write a sound.

b. Here's the sound you're going to write. Listen. **p**. What sound? (Signal.) *p*.

c. Write **p**. Check children's responses.

WORD WRITING

TASK 2   Children write **but**, **that**, **cat**

a. You're going to write the word **but**. Think about the sounds in (pause) **but** and write the word. Check children's responses.

To correct	1. Say the sounds in **but**. (Signal.) *Buuut*.
	2. Say the sounds the hard way. (Signal.) *B* (pause) *uuu* (pause) *t*.
	3. Write the word **but**. Check children's responses.

b. Repeat *a* for **that** and **cat**.

TASK 3   Children write **will**

a. You're going to write the word (pause) **will**. Say the sounds you write for (pause) **will**. Get ready. Signal for each sound as the children say *www* (pause) *iii* (pause) *lll* (pause) *lll*. The children are to pause two seconds between the sounds. Repeat until firm.

b. Everybody, write the word (pause) **will**. Check children's responses.

TASK 4   Children write **see**

You're going to write the word **see**. Think about the sounds in (pause) **see** and write the word. Check children's responses.

| To correct | 1. Say the sounds the hard way. (Signal.) *Sss* (pause) *ēēē* (pause) *ēēē*. |
| | 2. Write the word **see**. Check children's responses. |

SENTENCE WRITING

TASK 5 Children write a sentence

a. Listen to this sentence. **This car is tan**. Your turn. Say that sentence. Get ready. (Signal.) *This car is tan.*

b. Now you're going to say it the slow way. Get ready. Signal for each word as the children say *this* (pause) *car* (pause) *is* (pause) *tan.* Repeat until firm.

c. Everybody, write the sentence. Spell each word the right way.

Check children's responses.

END OF SPELLING LESSON

Spelling Lesson 76

SOUND WRITING

TASK 1 Children write p

a. You're going to write a sound.

b. Here's the sound you're going to write. Listen. **p**. What sound? (Signal.) *p.*

c. Write **p**. Check children's responses.

WORD WRITING

TASK 2 Children write bill

a. You're going to write the word (pause) **bill**. When you write the word (pause) **bill**, you write these sounds. **B** (pause) **iii** (pause) **lll** (pause) **lll**.

b. Say the sounds you write for (pause) **bill**. Signal for each sound as the children say *b* (pause) *iii* (pause) *lll* (pause) *lll*. The children are to pause two seconds between the sounds. Repeat until firm.

c. Everybody, write the word (pause) **bill**. Check children's responses.

TASK 3 Children write will

a. You're going to write the word (pause) **will**. Say the sounds you write for (pause) **will**. Get ready. Signal for each sound as the children say *www* (pause) *iii* (pause) *lll* (pause) *lll*. The children are to pause two seconds between the sounds. Repeat until firm.

b. Everybody, write the word (pause) **will**. Check children's responses.

TASK 4 Children write are, the, but

a. You're going to write the word **are**. Think about the sounds in (pause) **are** and write the word. Check children's responses.

To correct	1. Say the sounds the hard way. (Signal.) *Aaa* (pause) *rrr* (pause) *ēēē.*
	2. Write the word **are**. Check children's responses.

b. You're going to write the word **thē**. Think about the sounds in (pause) **thē** and write the word. Check children's responses.

To correct	1. Say the sounds in **thē**. (Signal.) *Thththēēē.*
	2. Say the sounds the hard way. (Signal.) *Ththth* (pause) *ēēē.*
	3. Write the word **thē**. Check children's responses.

c. Repeat *b* for **but**.

SENTENCE WRITING

TASK 5 Children write a sentence

a. Listen to this sentence. **It is a fat ant**. Your turn. Say that sentence. Get ready. (Signal.) *It is a fat ant.*

b. Now you're going to say it the slow way. Get ready. Signal for each word as the children say *it* (pause) *is* (pause) *a* (pause) *fat* (pause) *ant.* Repeat until firm.

c. Everybody, write the sentence. Spell each word the right way.

Check children's responses.

END OF SPELLING LESSON

Spelling Lesson 77

WORD WRITING

TASK 1   Children write **see**

You're going to write the word **see**. Think about the sounds in (pause) **see** and write the word. Check children's responses.

To correct	1. Say the sounds in **see**. (Signal.) *Sssēēē*.
	2. Say the sounds the hard way. (Signal.) *Sss* (pause) *ēēē* (pause) *ēēē*.
	3. Write the word **see**. Check children's responses.

TASK 2   Children write **barn, bill, pill**

a. You're going to write the word (pause) **barn**. Say the sounds you write for (pause) **barn**. Get ready. Signal for each sound as the children say *b* (pause) *aaa* (pause) *rrr* (pause) *nnn*. The children are to pause two seconds between the sounds. Repeat until firm.

b. Everybody, write the word (pause) **barn**. Check children's responses.

c. Now you're going to write the word (pause) **bill**. Say the sounds you write for (pause) **bill**. Get ready. Signal for each sound as the children say *b* (pause) *iii* (pause) *lll* (pause) *lll*. The children are to pause two seconds between the sounds. Repeat until firm.

d. Everybody, write the word (pause) **bill**. Check children's responses.

e. Next you're going to write the word (pause) **pill**. Say the sounds you write for (pause) **pill**. Get ready. Signal for each sound as the children say *p* (pause) *iii* (pause) *lll* (pause) *lll*. The children are to pause two seconds between the sounds. Repeat until firm.

f. Everybody, write the word (pause) **pill**. Check children's responses.

TASK 3   Children write **it**

You're going to write the word **it**. Think about the sounds in (pause) **it** and write the word. Check children's responses.

TASK 4   Children write **pit**

a. You're going to write the word **pit**. Listen. **Pit**. Saying the sounds in (pause) **pit** the hard way. Get ready. Signal for each sound as the children say *p* (pause) *iii* (pause) *t*. The children are to pause two seconds between the sounds. Repeat until firm.

b. Everybody, write the word (pause) **pit**. Check children's responses.

SENTENCE WRITING

TASK 5   Children write a sentence

a. Listen to this sentence. **We will win a car**. Your turn. Say that sentence. Get ready. (Signal.) *We will win a car*.

b. Now you're going to say it the slow way. Get ready. Signal for each word as the children say *we* (pause) *will* (pause) *win* (pause) *a* (pause) *car*. Repeat until firm.

c. Everybody, write the sentence. Spell each word the right way. Check children's responses.

END OF SPELLING LESSON

Spelling Lesson 78

WORD WRITING

TASK 1   Children write **bar, pill, will**

a. You're going to write the word (pause) **bar**. Say the sounds you write for (pause) **bar**. Get ready. Signal for each sound as the children say *b* (pause) *aaa* (pause) *rrr.* The children are to pause two seconds between the sounds. Repeat until firm.

b. Everybody, write the word (pause) **bar**. Check children's responses.

c. Now you're going to write the word (pause) **pill**. Say the sounds you write for (pause) **pill**. Get ready. Signal for each sound as the children say *p* (pause) *iii* (pause) *lll* (pause) *lll.* The children are to pause two seconds between the sounds. Repeat until firm.

d. Everybody, write the word (pause) **pill**. Check children's responses.

e. Next you're going to write the word (pause) **will**. Say the sounds you write for (pause) **will**. Get ready. Signal for each sound as the children say *www* (pause) *iii* (pause) *lll* (pause) *lll.* The children are to pause two seconds between the sounds. Repeat until firm.

f. Everybody, write the word (pause) **will**. Check children's responses.

TASK 2   Children write **ham, bit, land**

a. You're going to write the word **ham**. Think about the sounds in (pause) **ham** and write the word. Check children's responses.

To correct	1. Say the sounds in **ham**. (Signal.) *Haaammm.*
	2. Say the sounds the hard way. (Signal.) *H* (pause) *aaa* (pause) *mmm.*
	3. Write the word **ham**. Check children's responses.

b. Repeat *a* for **bit** and **land**.

SENTENCE WRITING

TASK 3   Children write a sentence

a. Listen to this sentence. **He had mud on him**. Your turn. Say that sentence. Get ready. (Signal.) *He had mud on him.*

b. Now you're going to say it the slow way. Get ready. Signal for each word as the children say *he* (pause) *had* (pause) *mud* (pause) *on* (pause) *him.* Repeat until firm.

c. Everybody, write the sentence. Spell each word the right way.

Check children's responses.

END OF SPELLING LESSON

Spelling Lesson 79

WORD WRITING

TASK 1   Children write **but**

You're going to write the word **but**. Think about the sounds in (pause) **but** and write the word. Check children's responses.

To correct	1. Say the sounds in **but**. (Signal.) *Buuut.*
	2. Say the sounds the hard way. (Signal.) *B* (pause) *uuu* (pause) *t.*
	3. Write the word **but**. Check children's responses.

TASK 2   Children write **bar**

a. You're going to write the word (pause) **bar**. Say the sounds you write for (pause) **bar**. Get ready. Signal for each sound as the children say *b* (pause) *aaa* (pause) *rrr.* The children are to pause two seconds between the sounds. Repeat until firm.

b. Everybody, write the word (pause) **bar**. Check children's responses.

TASK 3 Children write **his, see, barn, and**

a. You're going to write the word **his**. Think about the sounds in
  (pause) **his** and write the word. Check children's responses.

To correct	**1.** Say the sounds the hard way. (Signal.)
	H (pause) *iii* (pause) *sss*.
	2. Write the word **his**. Check children's responses.

b. You're going to write the word **see**. Think about the sounds in
  (pause) **see** and write the word. Check children's responses.

To correct	**1.** Say the sounds in **see**. (Signal.) *Sssēē̄*.
	2. Say the sounds the hard way. (Signal.)
	Sss (pause) *ēēē* (pause) *ēēē*.
	3. Write the word **see**. Check children's responses.

c. Repeat *a* for **barn**.
d. Repeat *b* for **and**.

SENTENCE WRITING

TASK 4 Children write a sentence

a. Listen to this sentence. **We are on the farm**. Your turn. Say that
  sentence. Get ready. (Signal.) *We are on the farm*.
b. Now you're going to say it the slow way. Get ready. Signal for
  each word as the children say *we* (pause) *are* (pause) *on* (pause)
  the (pause) *farm*. Repeat until firm.
c. Everybody, write the sentence. Spell each word the right way.
  Check children's responses.

END OF SPELLING LESSON 79

After completing Spelling Lesson 79, the children
should be placed in *Spelling Mastery*, Level A.